HOW DO YOU MANAGE?

HOW DO YOU MANAGE?

John Nicholson

BBC BOOKS

Published by BBC Books,
a division of BBC Enterprises Limited,
Woodlands, 80 Wood Lane, London W12 0TT
First published 1992
© John Nicholson 1992
ISBN 0 563 36311 8 H/B
ISBN 0 563 36335 5 P/B
Set in 10/13pt Century Old Style by Goodfellow & Egan Ltd, Cambridge
Printed and bound in Great Britain by Redwood Press Ltd, Melksham
Cover printed by Clays Ltd, St Ives plc.

Contents

Contents

Chapter 4   The clever stuff   86

Problem-solving – Barriers to creative thinking – Mindsets – Making yourself more creative – Using logic – Why you get decisions wrong – Learning from experience – Innovation

Chapter 5   Making it happen   112

Why do things *not* happen? – The art of influence – Selling ideas – Reports, presentations, meetings – How to negotiate – What to do when things *don't* happen – Managing conflict and crisis – Living to fight another day

Chapter 6   Walking the tightrope   138

Becoming comfortable with Crazy Time – Learning to love stress – Balancing your life – Acquiring the necessary life skills – Preparing for tomorrow's world – How *will* you manage?

Preface

Dr John Nicholson taught Psychology at the universities of Oxford, Reading and London, before setting up the Business Psychology Consultancy of which he is now Chairman. He is the author of ten books, five of which have had a TV series based on them, and several hundred articles.

John Nicholson Associates has worked in some 80 organisations, ranging in size from 40 to 300000 employees, covering most sectors of industry: for example, petrochemicals, communications, transport and distribution, financial services, airlines and motor industry, I.T., manufacturing, service, leisure, hotels and catering, and government organisations – central and local. Projects vary enormously in scope and focus, but the central objective is always the same: to unlock the human potential within client organisations. Sometimes, JNA consultants operate at a corporate level: for example, helping a board of directors redefine their strategic aims or offering a coaching/counselling service to a chief executive during a particularly testing period of growth or restructuring. More often, they work with teams, improving the quality of communication and cooperation or helping resolve inter-departmental wrangles. They also challenge individuals to rethink the purpose of their work and the effectiveness of their working methods, giving them the power to make their jobs work for them and encouraging people to achieve a better balance between professional success and personal happiness.

Conflict and stress are familiar aspects of corporate life. Business psychologists believe that they can be a valuable source of creative energy instead of merely a disruptive influence. Change and innovation, too, have become an inevitable part of working life in today's swiftly shifting business environment. Almost all John Nicholson Associates' assignments involve helping people become comfortable with fresh ways of thinking, different ways of operating, and new attitudes – towards colleagues, customers and the whole business of work.

Acknowledgements

Many people have shaped my thinking on the issues discussed in this book. Pride of place belongs to the thousands of men and women who, over the past decade, have invited me to help them develop their management skills. Their honesty, good humour and enthusiasm for new ideas have been an inspiration. I also owe an enormous debt to the friends and colleagues, past and present, who have been so generous with their time and ideas, and so tolerant of my idiosyncrasies. Heartfelt thanks to: Peter Berners-Price, Tessa Blackstone, Mark Brown, Sheila Chown, Arnold Cragg, Chris Devereux, Pat Dixon, Ian Farnfield, Carmen Harris, Adam Hilton, Jan Holmes, Susan Iacovou, Lois Jacobs, John McBride, Sandy McGillivray, Clare Mansfield, Peter Martin, Linda Phillimore, Bill Quirk, Michael Reddy, Diana Rice, Victor Rothschild and Kay Scott. Cathy Walton led the research effort and Fiona Thompson sailed serenely through the sub-editing.

But the book has to be dedicated to Daniel Alexander Nicholson who, at the age of three, manages me more effectively than the rest of them put together.

Introduction

This is a book about managing – not just other people, but yourself and your business. It's often said that a business has only two major assets: people and money. I am a psychologist, so I focus firmly on the people side. Of course, money needs to be managed too, and every successful organisation tries to keep costs down. But I can't accept that effective management is simply about reducing head count. People aren't just a cost. Those who no longer work for you can't be earning for you, never mind the effect their dismissal may have on the morale of their former colleagues. So, although getting rid of people can make the bottom line look healthier in the short term, it can never be a satisfactory recipe for long-term commercial success.

If that sounds like special pleading, it's because most of my working life is spent advising companies on how to keep people in work, by helping them make the most of their human resources. I do this by persuading people at every level, from boardroom to shop floor, to think again about their everyday working practices and about the spirit in which they carry out their jobs. Sometimes I need to suggest new ways of operating, but more often it turns out that people already have all the know-how they need to work better, tucked away in their brains. All I have to do is get it to the top of their heads, and on to their 'to do' list. This is achieved by giving them sufficient thinking time and creating an atmosphere in which people feel that it's safe to explore new ideas, admit to mistakes and learn from each other's experiences.

How do you Manage? is written from the point of view of a business psychologist, but if you're after high-flown theorising, it's not the book for you. This is a practical, working book. It is written to *involve*, as well as inform you, and it has a strong Do-It-Yourself flavour. There are many quizzes and exercises to be carried out, either on your own or with colleagues. I shall analyse why things go wrong and suggest ways of putting them right. My aim is to explain why you do some of the things you do as a manager, and suggest ways in which you could perform your job more effectively and more enjoyably by making relatively small changes in your way of operating.

The logic of *How do you Manage?* is straightforward. It starts from the assumption that before you can manage anyone effectively, you must first have a realistic idea of what sort of person you are and how other people see you. This process should include an appreciation of your own significant strengths and weaknesses, and a pragmatic assessment of any changes you need to make to become a more effective manager.

Consider the following 10 principles of good management practice. Read them carefully, think through their implications, then ask yourself how many of them you break, and how often.

1   Accept that you are the one person you can actually change – other people can only be shown the possibilities, and given a helping hand.
2   If you haven't got enough time, blame yourself.
3   Respect other people's views and allow them to be different from you – you may be wrong.
4   Don't select people because they remind you of yourself – cloning limits the options of the team.
5   Never assume that they heard what you said – or that you understood what they really meant.
6   Catch people doing things well – and praise them.
7   Make problems pay for the trouble they cause – by forcing them to show you how to avoid them in future.
8   Before trying to persuade anyone of anything, first convince yourself.
9   Make it easy for people to give you what you want.
10 Don't live in the past – it wasn't like you remember, and it's never coming back.   ●

Don't be surprised if this exercise makes you uneasy. Some of my principles may strike you as unrealistic or even unfair. Surely only thoughtless bosses or incompetent colleagues leave you short of time

– and why on earth should you feel responsible when people don't listen properly to what you are saying?

The 10 principles will give you a flavour of my approach. *How do you Manage?* is a selfish book, in the best sense of the word. I believe you have a lot more power to influence events around you than you may realise, and that you should use all legitimate means to advance your views and your own best interests. In my experience of organisations, the most successful have been those which devolve authority and responsibility as widely and as far down as possible. People in these organisations perform to the best of their ability most of the time, not just because they feel truly accountable for what they do, but because they are able to experience the organisation's success as if it were their own. It's my observation that almost everyone, given a real choice, prefers to do their job well rather than badly, whatever the job may be. I also find that people are delighted by the suggestion that they should try to make their job work for them, rather than the other way round.

You could read the title of this book with four different emphases. All are revealing. For example, ***How** do you Manage?* emphasises the book's practical slant. *How **do** you Manage?* acknowledges that it is not easy to be an effective manager. *How do **you** Manage?* makes the point that management is a flexible art, best accomplished by individuals who know themselves well and have devised ways of operating that suit their own personalities, and exploit their strengths. *How do you **Manage?*** focuses the spotlight on our essential subject matter. As I said at the beginning, this is a book about managing. Enjoy it!

Chapter 1

Who do you think you are?

To manage other people successfully, you must understand what sort of person you are and how other people see you. If you don't, your motives are likely to be misinterpreted and your messages misunderstood. But if you do, you've taken the first step towards the managerial version of Utopia – a world in which people do what you want them to, not because you've told them to, but because it's what they want to do. So the first rule of management must be: know yourself.

But what particular aspects of yourself do you have to be aware of? Here are seven key questions. Think about them and see how confident you are in your ability to answer them.

1   What do you really want?
2   What are you really capable of?
3   How much do you like yourself?
4   Why do other people see you the way they do?
5   How content are you in your job?
6   Do you really want to take responsibility for your life?
7   Do you want to change – and can you do it?

How well do you know yourself? You might find it helpful to check reality by talking through your answers with someone who knows you well – your partner, perhaps, or a friend or work colleague – and discuss any differences of opinion.

There's another exercise which shows to what extent your thinking is in tune with other people's. Sit down with a group of people who know you and get everyone to write down a paragraph about themselves. Avoid referring to anything that would distinguish you from the group – physical characteristics, events etc. Collect the descriptions and redistribute them at random. Then get each person to read out their allocated paragraph. The object is for each person to see if they can identify the author. You actually learn two things from this exercise: how people you know well see themselves, and how they imagine you see yourself.

Both these exercises are about subjective impressions, your own and other people's. Personal impressions are based on how you think and feel. Where other people are concerned, you have to interpret what they do and say. You can only guess how they're feeling, so differences of opinion become inevitable. It may come as an unpleasant surprise to discover some of the things other people think about you. When this happens, there are three different ways you can react:

● you are so confident in yourself and your own judgement that you dismiss out of hand opinions that disagree with yours;

● you have so little confidence that you accept their view without question and become even more uncertain of your own judgement;

● you disagree, but find the other views sufficiently interesting to start a discussion to find out where the truth lies, as well as why the discrepancy has arisen.

Which of these responses is closest to yours? No prizes for guessing which one gains the psychologist's seal of approval!

Now, let's unpack each of the seven key questions, to find out why they're important and then explore some techniques for putting you more in touch with yourself, and turning this knowledge to practical use.

What do you really want?

Here is an exercise to discover what really matters to you. Scan through the following list of life values and rank them in order of their importance to you today in the 'Now' column (1 for most important, 11 for least). Then think back to five years ago and draw up a league table of what mattered most to you then. Rack your brains to reconstruct what your priorities were, and fill in the 'Then' column (again, using 1 for most important, 11 for least).

	RANKING	
	NOW	THEN
Leadership *To become an influential leader; or organise and control others to achieve community or organisational goals.*	☐	☐
Expertness *To become an authority on a special subject; to persevere to reach an expert level of skill and accomplishment.*	☐	☐
Prestige *To become well-known/obtain recognition, awards or high social status.*	☐	☐
Service *To contribute to the satisfaction of others; to be helpful to others who need it.*	☐	☐
Wealth *To earn a great deal of money; to build up a large financial estate.*	☐	☐
Independence *To have freedom of thought and action; to be your own boss.*	☐	☐
Affection *To obtain and share companionship and affection through immediate family and friends.*	☐	☐
Security *To achieve a secure and stable position in work and financial situations.*	☐	☐
Self-realisation *To optimise personal development; to realise your full creative and innovative potential.*	☐	☐
Duty *To dedicate yourself totally to the pursuit of ultimate values, ideas and principles.*	☐	☐
Pleasure *To enjoy life, to be happy and content, to have the good things in life.*	☐	☐

When you've done this, look at the differences between your 'Now' and 'Then' columns. What does it say about you and your changing ambitions? Now look ahead. Imagine a day at work in about two years' time. The day is perfect in the sense that it includes in it all of the things you would like your ideal day to involve. Describe in detail what this day would be like.

Think about

- location

- the type of work you would be doing

- the sort/range of people you would be working with

- how hard you would be working

- the size and structure of the company.

Which parts of this day would you value most? In what way does this day differ from the present reality of your work, best and worst days? If you want to take this exercise to its logical conclusion, you can also think of what a particularly bad day for you at work two years down the track might be like. Again, list the factors that would make the day so unpleasant.

It's true to say that, 'You can't always get what you want'. However, most successful managers aim to organise their jobs so as to maximise the many psychological benefits that work can offer. The name of the game is 'making your job work for you', rather than vice versa. It's a skill worth mastering, since it enhances job satisfaction, makes you feel better about yourself, removes an irritating source of discontent and generally creates a state of mind in which it becomes possible to operate most effectively.

One thing is certain: the first step towards getting what you want out of work has to be identifying your requirements and accepting that they will probably change over time. The importance of money, for example, varies enormously from one stage of life to another. So you'll need to check at regular intervals that you aren't pursuing yesterday's dreams, and be prepared to shift priorities at work and elsewhere to ensure that you've still got the right fit between you and your work.

What are you really capable of?

Many managers have the feeling that they're not really making the most of their abilities. They are either over-familiar with the job (does five years in the same job equal five years' experience or one year repeated five times?) or they haven't yet managed to find a job which uses all their skills. Psychologists tell us that most people never use more than a fraction of their intellectual potential (more on this in Chapter 4). Emotionally, too, we are the victims of early experiences which can lumber us with a set of irrational and limiting assumptions. For example, a woman I once knew told me about a critical incident in her early childhood. Her class at school were given the opportunity to make a present for their fathers. There was a choice – they could make either a model Catherine wheel or a heron. That evening, bursting with pride, she told her father the story and presented him with a crude but recognisable Catherine wheel. She remembers him looking at it for what seemed an eternity. Then he cleared his throat and said: 'A heron would have been nice.'

A host of similar incidents in childhood led her to draw two conclusions: that she is no good at making decisions; and that men are impossible to please. As adults, many of us are the victims of such assumptions, based on childhood experience and reinforced by feedback received from powerful adults such as parents and teachers. Below, you will see five of the most common assumptions, all of which create false expectations and hence lead inevitably to disappointment. As a result, they are self-perpetuating. They give a false perspective on the world, particularly where other people's motivations are concerned, and can lead to some pretty self-destructive behaviour.

Although all five assumptions are ill-founded, it's not easy to eliminate their influence unless you are alert to certain tell-tale phrases, and give yourself regular doses of the appropriate antidotes.

Five fatal assumptions

Assumption 1

I must perform perfectly, always and in all respects.

Tell-tale phrases

'Why do I never get things right?'
'You're only saying that to be kind.'

Antidote

You need to re-programme your thinking here along the following lines. No one is perfectly competent at anything all the time, let alone at everything. You do, however, have certain attributes you can be proud of and things that you do better than most people. It may be worth listing them, fighting the false modesty that is so often an obstacle to self-esteem.

Assumption 2

Everyone must love me and approve of everything I do.

Tell-tale phrases

'But if I do that, it's going to make someone very unhappy.'
'I thought you were my friend. By not supporting me on this issue, you are betraying me.'

Antidote

It's a fact of life that you can't please all the people all the time because different people have different interests. Any decision is bound to displease someone, which is why Assumption 2 sufferers find decision-making so painful. Assumption 2 can also trigger off two damaging further assumptions: either 'There's something dreadfully wrong with me'; or 'It's all *their* fault'. You need to boost your self-confidence to the point where loss of one person's approval is really neither here nor there.

Assumption 3

I have a right to expect other people to give me everything I want.

Tell-tale phrases

'Why won't they give me a break?'
'Why is everybody against me?'

Antidote

Not only do you have no right to expect it, but this assumption is the very antithesis of the way an effective manager's mind works. Experience teaches us that we never get everything we want from other people. There are many times when other people can't – and probably shouldn't – give you what you ask them for. People who don't give you what you want may have an excellent reason for their behaviour. They have their own lives to run, their own pressures, and their own deadlines and concerns. It's most unlikely that they hate you.

Assumption 4

I am the product and the victim of my personal history.

Tell-tale phrases

'I never had a chance, really, did I?'
'But this is what I/they always do.'

Antidote

Of course your past must have an effect on who you are today. However, you are not stuck with it. People develop and change spontaneously. It is open to anyone to seek to speed up or shape the process. We will say more about this later in the chapter. For the present, be assured that there is a vast research literature documenting successful, self-directed personal change programmes, ranging from the Book of Genesis through to last week's football results. The problem is that we are more likely to notice the failures than the successes when we have made worthy resolutions. It may be a worthwhile exercise to keep a success diary, in which you note everything that happens at work the way you planned it.

Assumption 5

When I am unhappy it's always someone else's fault.

Tell-tale phrases

'Why do they always pick on me?'
'I knew it was too good to last.'

Antidote

Blaming other people for your unhappiness gives you an excuse not to make an effort to put things right. By projecting your feelings on to them and wasting your energy devising schemes to get revenge for imagined wrongs, you are simply postponing the hunt for solutions. Solving other people's problems is a classic example of displacement activity, i.e. doing something futile and irrelevant when there is a necessary but difficult task to be accomplished.

Of course, not all the constraints on a manager's effectiveness stem from past experience. Everyday working life is full of distractions and obstacles that prevent most of us from functioning as effectively as we feel we could. But, rather than focus exclusively on the downside, we should now look briefly at personal strengths, since self-aware managers try to play to their strengths as well as take steps to remedy weaknesses.

A number of organisations have tried to establish what qualities successful managers have in common. The usual technique is to compare a group of high-performing managers with a group of those who are barely up to par, in order to establish the characteristics that distinguish them. Unfortunately, the outcome of this kind of research is not clear-cut. Different organisations require different qualities from their high-flyers. The intellectual skill most consistently linked with managerial success is known as 'helicopter vision' – the ability to see the big picture, integrate all the parts, see a situation from several different points of view and operate at a purely conceptual level, having isolated the essential issues of the problem. Where people-handling skills are concerned, it is possible to identify a number of key elements. You will get a chance to see how you measure up to them in Chapter 2.

For the moment, though, we are concerned with the more general problems of feeling either that you are not making the most of your ability, or the opposite – that you are being asked to do things beyond your capability, or are landed with a workload so excessive that you are unable to cope. Two useful techniques can be applied to both situations.

The first device, known as Putting Problems in Perspective, is designed to prevent several tasks, that separately are quite simple, coming together to form a mental agglomeration that feels too oppressive even to contemplate. You need simply to break down all the tasks which confront you into component parts, give each a separate identity, then assess each in turn for complexity and the time required to deal with it.

The second technique is based on Critical Incident Analysis. The trick here is to focus on episodes from your recent working life in which you feel you have acquitted yourself unusually well or embarrassingly ineffectively. You need to put pen to paper to describe each one in detail, paying particular attention to whatever aspects of your own performance you feel particularly proud or ashamed of. On the basis of a number of these incidents, you should be able to draw up a reasonably objective list of your personal strengths and weaknesses.

You can use the list of strengths as an immediate confidence booster. Of course, it should also be the basis for all action planning, to ensure that you make the most of your positive attributes. The catalogue of personal weaknesses, on the other hand, can become the basis of an effective programme of remedial action. Are there critical skills you need to acquire or sharpen up? Attitudes you need to re-think? Working relationships that need to be reassessed or working methods that are no longer appropriate? And since the world isn't going to stop while you improve yourself, it may be that colleagues could be used more effectively to cover for the weaknesses you have identified in yourself, until such time as you have remedied them.

How much do you like yourself?

Many unsuccessful managers suffer from an excessive need to be liked. This prevents them from making hard but necessary decisions, and ironically often results in them being disliked – the very thing they are most anxious to avoid. But it also seems to be true that some less successful people-handlers have a rather different problem: they dislike themselves. This puts them at a severe disadvantage, since self-respect is a necessary condition for the respect that every successful manager needs to command from their team.

Here is an exercise to give you an idea of how good you feel about yourself. Make a list of 10 people who play a significant part in your life (friends, relatives or colleagues, for example). Include yourself among the list of names and write each one on a postcard. Then think about the contribution that all these people make to life on the planet. Because there is an almost infinite number of ways in which this can be measured, it won't be a tidy or an easy process. You may even find it uncomfortable. But persevere, accepting that the task is a subjective one and will almost certainly involve an element of injustice. Reassure yourself that it is only an exercise – no one is actually going to suffer as a result of your decisions! Arrange the cards in a sequence with the least valuable person on the left, ascending to the most valuable on the right. The only card that actually matters is the one containing your own name. Its position in the sequence will give you a rough indication of the current level of your self-esteem.

Past and present failures, and frustrations, at home and at work, can undermine the view you have of yourself. Success, and other people's appreciation, have the opposite effect. You can get a more accurate fix on the balance between these two conflicting pressures by answering the following questions.

		TRUE	FALSE
1	*I reckon I can do things as well as most people.*	☑	☐
2	*It's not easy being me.*	☐	☑
3	*When I have to make a presentation, I'm terrified of making a fool of myself.*	☐	☑
4	*It's not often that I think of myself as a failure.*	☑	☐
5	*There are lots of things about myself I'd change if I could.*	☑	☐
6	*I am rarely bothered by other people's criticism.*	☐	☑
7	*Other people tend to be more well-liked than I am.*	☐	☑
8	*If I have something to say, I usually go ahead and say it.*	☑	☐
9	*I don't often feel ashamed of anything I have done.*	☑	☐
10	*When people say complimentary things about me, I find it hard to believe they really mean it.*	☑	☐

Score two points for each 'True' answer to questions 1, 4, 6, 8, and 9; score zero for every 'False' answer. For questions 2, 3, 5, 7 and 10, score two points for each 'False'; score zero for each 'True' answer.

The higher your score, the better the opinion you have of yourself. A score of 14 or more suggests that you are quite confident; not necessarily conceited, but you certainly like yourself well enough, and there's no danger of other people being made to feel uncomfortable by any signs of self-loathing in you.

A score of 8 or less suggests that you have serious doubts about yourself and your value to the world. It may of course be a temporary state of affairs – perhaps the result of some recent misfortune. But if this is your normal condition, other people are bound to pick it up, and the risk is that they will accept your low estimate of yourself and hence find it difficult to respect you.

Why do other people see you the way they do?

Much of the discussion so far has been about the sort of person you are – your strengths and weaknesses, skills and attributes, attitudes and personality – as if this is a constant, unchanging, universally accepted phenomenon. But of course, it's not. People don't behave consistently in all situations, and you can't predict exactly how anyone will behave in a given situation – even yourself! Other people have to interpret what you do and can only guess what is going on in your mind. And of course you are subject to exactly the same limitations when trying to make sense of their behaviour.

So far as situations are concerned, some contexts have rules and conventions which sometimes force you to behave uncharacteristically. If you are in a meeting with colleagues, you are obliged to take your turn in the conversation and to listen to what they have to say. In an interview, there are different rules to be followed by the people playing each of the two roles: interviewer and person being interviewed. You could find yourself filling both roles at different times in the same day, in which case you would have to behave rather differently, even though you remained one and the same person.

We are obliged to play a host of different roles: competent boss, loyal subordinate, caring parent, dutiful child, stimulating partner, law-abiding citizen and so on. Some of these roles are imposed on us; some fit us more comfortably than others. It's quite common to feel torn between the conflicting demands of two different roles. For example, role conflict can be a particular problem for working mothers. Women who wish to devote 100 per cent of their energy to their career, but have no desire to give any less to their family, are inevitably stymied by the arithmetic of the situation. They are not helped by the fact that, while more than half of the women in Britain have jobs outside the home, domestic cleaning and administration remain almost universally accepted as a woman's responsibility. Research indicates that women are significantly less content than men to accept a reduced commitment to the domestic role when it comes into conflict with work. However, women are also found to be more adept at switching their mental set in a way that allows them to attend to the priorities of a different role from the one they are currently adopting. This mental juggling act brings them close to squaring the circle. It allows women managers to survive the pressures of a double life, and it may give them an advantage over their male counterparts in complex business situations.

Roles carry responsibilities that clash with natural preferences. A naturally kind and compassionate manager, obliged by business reasons to fire a capable and blameless member of staff, might have to say things they would regard as utterly out of character. Job status and the distinction between home and office are two other areas in which we are constantly showing how flexible – and inconsistent – we can be. The dominant male boss who turns into the meek husband after work (and may even regress to childhood with his mother) has become a stereotype. At work it's common to witness a respectful, even obsequious, subordinate becoming an overbearing bully – in no more than the time it takes for a director to leave his office, and a junior member of staff to enter.

It's hardly surprising that other people sometimes have a strange impression of us. Occasionally, they have simply got it wrong. They may be suffering from the effects of history. Perhaps they haven't noticed that we are no longer the person we were when they first met us. For example, two former students of mine have become directors of my company. When I first met them, I was in the role of all-knowing teacher and they accorded me a respect I – but not they – knew I hardly deserved. Now that their psychological knowledge at least matches mine, we have all had to rethink our roles and attitudes towards each other. Along the way, there have been minor upsets and occasionally the old balance of power has reasserted itself. The change of circumstances has tested several of the principles being discussed here, and it has certainly brought home to me how powerful early impressions are, and how important it is not to take anything for granted in long-term working relationships.

Occasionally, other people are clearly at fault, perhaps because they simply confuse us with someone else. For example, I used to be irritated by a close friend's refusal to accept that I like baked beans. It was actually her father who had an aversion to them, and she wouldn't believe that we had different taste preferences! More seriously, sometimes it's our own fault when people misjudge us, because we allow misconceptions to form. We may even encourage them to suit our own purposes. We also forget that the same piece of behaviour can be interpreted in two very different ways, depending on whether you are the person performing or observing it.

As a manager you need to be alert to rival interpretations of common patterns of behaviour. For example, what I regard as the flexibility of my position, may strike you as inconsistency. Here is a list of other important motivational mismatches, when well-intentioned behaviour is subject to a much less charitable interpretation by those on the receiving end.

HOW I SEE MYSELF	HOW THEY SEE ME
confident	arrogant
enterprising	opportunistic
humorous	frivolous
ambitious	ruthless
helpful	controlling
forceful	bullying
competitive	combative
open to change	wishy-washy
thorough	obsessive
tolerant	uncaring
caring	nosy
prudent	indecisive
focused	tunnel-visioned
supportive	interfering
generous	irresponsible

You don't have to be a slave to other people's perceptions of you, but it is useful to understand and appreciate them. You can't hope to exert total control over how your actions are perceived. You should, however, always be alert to the possibility of misinterpretation, and it's a good idea to check from time to time that other people aren't misjudging you – especially when dealing with people you don't know very well. Even with people you know well, it's important to be aware of their preconceptions, and to challenge them if you feel they are resisting your attempts to change yourself.

This raises a final issue: other people's expectations. Just as we make unrealistic demands on them, so other people sometimes look for assistance we are unable or unwilling to provide. For example, you may have a subordinate who clearly requires a style of management that is alien to you. Failing to meet such expectations is always painful, though it's often the lesser of two evils. You can usually lessen their disappointment by explaining why you are unable to oblige, and the benefits of your preferred style of management. Accepting that you cannot please all the people all the time has to be one of the most important lessons a manager must learn.

How content are you in your job?

Just as managers with a low opinion of themselves have difficulty in commanding respect, so those who are unhappy in their job won't find it easy to motivate others. There will inevitably be aspects of your job you find frustrating, and particular days when the temptation to stay in bed is strong. This last observation gives rise to a useful rule of thumb, which can be applied by anyone in serious doubt as to their suitability for their current job. It's quite acceptable to wake up one morning and dread the prospect of going to work. But if you do so every day for a week, you should at least devote serious thought to what is causing your anxiety. There may be a specific problem that can be solved or is going to disappear spontaneously. But if the feeling is more general, and you can see no reason why it will change next week, it may be time to move on.

You can bring a little more precision to what must be a very serious decision by answering the following questions, which are designed to measure your job satisfaction.

		TRUE	FALSE
1	*If I won the pools, I certainly wouldn't carry on working where I am now.*	☐	☑
2	*The most important things that happen to me involve work.*	☑	☐
3	*I'm always looking for ways to do my job more effectively.*	☑	☐
4	*When I get into difficulty at work, there's no one I can turn to for help.*	☐	☑

	TRUE	FALSE
5 Even if another employer offered me a lot of money, I would not seriously think of changing my present job.	☑	☐
6 In all honesty, I couldn't advise a friend to join my company.	☐	☑
7 I often find myself looking back on a day's work with a sense of a job well done.	☑	☐
8 I am too embarrassed to tell people who I work for.	☐	☐
9 If I had my life over again, I wouldn't choose to do the job I'm doing.	☐	☑
10 It makes me unhappy when my work is not up to its usual standard.	☑	☐

Score two points for each 'True' answer to questions 2, 3, 5, 7 and 10, and zero for each 'False'. For questions 1, 4, 6, 8 and 9, score two points for each 'False', and zero for each 'True' answer.

The higher your score, the more satisfied you are. A score of 14 or more suggests that you find your job worth while – personally as well as financially. A score of 6 or less indicates that you are getting less pleasure from your work than most managers do – and less than is healthy for you.

In recessionary times, people are understandably nervous about giving up their jobs voluntarily, however dissatisfied they may be feeling. But consider the downside of *not* giving up a job to which you are thoroughly ill-suited. There is overwhelming evidence that work-related stress is not just health-threatening, but also affects all other areas of your life. Stress at work stems from many causes. For example, poor communications, a lack of control over working conditions, workload, the organisation of the immediate working environment, inadequate information about what is going on, and a management culture that leans heavily towards blame and away from praise. But the most stressful experience work has to offer is that of being a round peg in a square hole. We will look at stress in more detail in Chapter 6, but for now the problem is in deciding at what point you should stop trying to achieve a tolerable fit and cut your losses. It's a subjective judgement, and you may not know until much later whether or not you got the timing right.

Do you really want to take responsibility for your life?

We have just seen that the feeling of being unable to control your immediate working environment is a major source of work-related stress. Feeling helpless is related to profound psychological distress, severe illness, even death. Conversely, feeling competent and in control is a major source of job satisfaction. It is also related to successful planning for the future. Despite this, most of us have reservations about assuming sole responsibility for our own destiny. At times, we are only too happy to hide behind mysterious 'forces beyond our control', and to blame 'Them' when things go wrong. 'They' may be either colleagues or people who work for us. More often, though, it's the boss who gets blamed.

Here is a simple exercise to see whether or not you are ready to assume control of your own destiny at work. Write down the name of the person who causes you the most grief at work. What is it they do that annoys you most? Have you told them about it – in detail and with suggestions as to how you would prefer them to behave? If you haven't, why not? Are you satisfied with the explanation you have just given yourself?

The thought process you have just been through shouldn't have been a difficult one. It may, however, have made you uncomfortable, and it's quite a powerful test of how prepared you are to fight for the right to do your job your way, to the best of your ability. After all, you were asked to name the major obstacle in your working life. If you haven't taken steps to deal with that, you're probably not in the right frame of mind to take control in other areas.

One reason why you may not be able to take control is that you are scared of success. This may sound like a ridiculous idea in our society, where success and achievement are so highly valued. Although seeming to aim for these 'approved' goals, people may have underlying reasons which make them want to undermine their plans. For example, a city-based executive who secretly yearns for a life in the country may subconsciously jeopardise vital meetings and business relationships in an attempt to be forced out of the job and therefore the city. This slow and indirect means of achieving what you really want is called 'self-handicapping'. As a strategy for avoiding control, it is weak and by no means guarantees that you will get what you want. Unless you examine your motives and approach problem-solving in a positive frame of mind, you will not be in charge of the direction your life takes.

This frame of mind is described as 'empowerment', and it's a notion we shall have a lot to say about throughout this book. You can measure how empowered you are at present by answering the following questions.

		YES	NO
1	*Is there some habit, such as smoking, that you would like to break but cannot?*	☐	☑
2	*Generally speaking, would you say you got your fair share of life's breaks?*	☑	☐
3	*Do you believe your own personality was laid down firmly by childhood experiences, so that there is nothing you can do to change this?*	☑	☐
4	*Do you make your own decisions regardless of what other people say?*	☐	☑
5	*Do you find it a waste of time planning ahead because in the end something always turns up causing you to change your plans?*	☐	☑
6	*If something goes wrong at work, do you usually reckon it's your fault rather than just bad luck?*	☑	☐
7	*Do you find it difficult to say 'No' to people?*	☑	☐
8	*Do you often feel you are the victim of outside forces you cannot control?*	☐	☑
9	*Do you usually manage to resist being persuaded by other people's arguments?*	☑	☐
10	*Do you believe that getting to the top is mainly a question of ability and that luck doesn't really come into it?*	☐	☑

Score two points for each 'Yes' answer to questions 2, 4, 6, 9 and 10, and zero for 'No' replies. For questions 1, 3, 5, 7 and 8, score two points for every 'No' answer, and zero for 'Yes'.

If your score is 16 or more, you appear to be comfortably in control of events and happy to accept responsibility for both the more and the less successful outcomes of your activities. You are neither a buck-passer nor an embittered victim, and the chances are that you will be able to communicate the benefits of personal empowerment to other people. A score of 13–15 is marginal, while a score of 12 or less raises questions about the way you work and who you work for. Are you taking on too much and not delegating enough? Are there extra resources – in yourself or elsewhere in the organisation – which you should be looking to exploit in order to reduce the feeling of being at the mercy of events?

Do you want to change – and can you do it?

'Give me:
> the serenity to accept the things I cannot change
> the courage to change the things I can
> the wisdom to recognise the difference.'

Of course, it's not quite as simple as this. Some people have no desire to change, while different people have different ideas about what they consider is or is not possible. Many of the most successful entrepreneurs have been dismissed as impossible dreamers. Their life stories reveal that the road to huge success tends to be littered with painful failures (Henry Ford's early brushes with bankruptcy are probably the best-known example).

At the other extreme there are people who proudly describe themselves as pragmatists or realists. Such folk are past masters at adapting themselves to whatever situation they find themselves in. They are not ones for chancing their arm and they rarely fall flat on their faces. However, they do not often reach the top in today's business environment.

This is because we are living in a period of massive change which affects virtually every aspect of the world of work. The globalisation of markets and the socio-demographic trends that have produced a shortage of young qualified people are just two of the factors which lead to accepted wisdom being turned on its head: the decision not to change has been transformed from the safe option to the riskiest. The reason is very simple. People – like organisations – need to fit comfortably into the environment in which they operate. In a changing environment, the ability to adjust rapidly and effectively becomes the hallmark of the winner, as well as an essential attribute for survival.

For the foreseeable future, therefore, it seems that the race is going to belong to the swiftest to adapt, and hence that the most successful managers will be those who feel most comfortable with new ways of doing things.

The implication of all this is that if your answer to the question 'Do you want to change?' is 'No', and you are ambitious for success, you are in trouble! Here are some questions to help you discover how ready you are to embrace change.

		TRUE	FALSE
1	I often wish people would be more definite about things.	☑	☐
2	It's not always necessary to make sure that your work is carefully planned.	☐	☑
3	I do sympathise with people who can't make up their minds about what they really believe.	☐	☑
4	I think a well-ordered pattern of life, with regular hours, suits me best.	☐	☑
5	We'd be lost without words like 'probably', 'approximately' and 'perhaps'.	☐	☑
6	The trouble with many people is that they take things too seriously.	☑	☐
7	People who seem unsure or uncertain about the world make me feel uncomfortable.	☑	☐
8	I try to keep an open mind about things.	☑	☐
9	I always finish what I start.	☐	☑
10	I like to have a place for everything and everything in its place.	☐	☐

Score two points for each 'True' answer to questions 2, 3, 5, 6, and 8, and zero for every 'False'. For questions 1, 4, 7, 9 and 10, score two points for each 'False', and zero for every 'True' answer.

The higher your score, the more adaptable and the more open you are to new ways of doing things. A score of 18 or more makes you almost a change junkie! Fourteen or more points suggests that you are pretty well-equipped to handle change. A score of 7–13 is marginal, but you'll probably be able to cope with a reasonable amount of change. A score of 6 or less implies a degree of rigidity and a reluctance to consider alternatives to well-tried ways of doing things.

At present you are not at all comfortable with the process of change and probably remain unconvinced that it's necessary. I hope that this book will help convince you, because in a changing environment those who are unwilling to consider change run the risk of becoming an endangered species.

What makes self-improvement and real change possible is that so many of us use no more than a fraction of our potential. Anybody can improve their memory and their skills at getting on with other people. Similarly, concentration and stamina can be built up, and most bad habits can be unlearned – whatever your age – provided you really have the will to change and plan matters sensibly.

But before setting in motion a programme of self-change, you should check whether it is really you that needs to change, and not merely some aspect of your lifestyle. Following the earlier discussion, you may also need to decide between rounding off the corners of a peg to make a better fit and searching for a different-shaped hole!

Here are four principles that will help you change yourself.

1 *Don't be your own worst enemy!* Partners, colleagues and friends will often try to stop you changing yourself, because they are used to you as you are and feel threatened by you changing. However, the major enemy to change has to be your own attitude.

2 *Know yourself!* No two people are the same. We all have different needs and it is up to every individual to establish their own, and to do their best not to find themselves in a situation where they are either just pandering to someone else's wishes or trying to carry out a job according to guidelines designed with someone else in mind. You must establish how you work most effectively and try to create a work-style which allows you to function best – provided, of course, it is not in complete conflict with those around you.

3 *Don't underestimate yourself or your capacity to change!* Never accept other people's estimation of you passively.

4 *Give yourself a break!* Get inside other people's heads and be prepared to educate them to your way of doing things. Take problems seriously, but don't make totally unrealistic demands on yourself. Don't be afraid to accept responsibility. Human

beings suffer more from having too little responsibility in their lives than too much.

Reassure yourself that change is possible, provided you choose the right things to alter and set about doing so realistically. For example, research shows that 97 per cent of those who try to lose weight, weigh as much, or even more, 12 months later. But this does not mean that weight loss is impossible. Most people who go on a diet simply don't need to. They are not medically overweight and so are being unrealistic. More importantly, we know that severe dieting is a very inefficient way to lose weight. So most dieters have chosen both the wrong thing to change and the wrong way of changing it!

It is very difficult, if not impossible, to change fairly major aspects of your personality. However, most people simply want to change aspects of their behaviour or the feelings they have about them. For example, a very shy person could live with their shyness if it did not make them clam up when confronted by a stranger. This particular behavioural change is one that is quite possible to make. Identifying specific characteristics that are currently a source of weakness and either neutralising them by understanding or turning them into a positive virtue by re-directing them, is the sort of change everyone is capable of making. Often, merely understanding why you do something gives you the power to control it.

One way to handle personal change is to regard it as a three-stage conversion. In the first part, you look ahead and imagine what you will be like when you have changed. For example, one reason why many fat people find it difficult to lose weight is that they do not anticipate what life will be like as a thin person, and panic as they realise that many of the defences open to the fat person will now be closed to them – for example, being a 'joker'. In the second stage, you must behave as if you are already the person you'd like to be. This is a role-playing exercise. Of course you are not yet the new person, but you will get the feel of that person by adopting the trappings of the part. The third stage of change is arrived at when this role playing becomes reality. Often it is a gradual process, a matter of losing self-consciousness and no longer asking whether this person who is refusing a cigarette or insisting on their rights being respected can really be you. Here is a checklist to help you make change a reality.

Checklist for change

●   Commit yourself to the idea that change is possible.

●   Explore your reasons for wanting to change.

●   Check how well you know yourself.

●   Decide exactly what it is that needs to be changed. Is it you or just some aspect of your lifestyle?

●   Make sure you understand and are prepared for the likely consequences of change.

●   Set yourself a series of modest, short-term goals, rather than going for the jack-pot from the beginning.

●   Make sure the change is something you can start on right now. The *mañana* spirit is fatal to successful change.

●   Avoid negative thinking. Don't talk yourself into failure, and avoid unrealistic strategies and people who are unlikely to help you succeed. Don't be discouraged by other people's responses, and don't make too much of temporary setbacks.

●   Keep a constant check on how well you are doing. Reward yourself for successes, either by allowing yourself a treat or, better, by simple self-congratulation. Get other people who are sympathetic to what you are doing to help too.

This chapter has been about understanding yourself and learning how to make the most of your abilities. I have tried to convince you that successful managers seek control over what happens to themselves, their people and their immediate environment. In today's business climate, the ability to manage change is at a premium. We shall return to this vital concern in Chapters 5 and 6.

Chapter 2

So you want to be a better manager?

Now you know a bit more about yourself, and have a clearer idea of how other people see you, you are ready to contemplate the art of managing – both yourself and them. In this chapter we shall be looking at the skills needed for managing individuals. The problems associated with managing teams will be dealt with in Chapter 3. For now, here are some key questions.

1 How good a manager are you?
2 What do good managers do?
3 Why is it difficult to be a good manager?
4 Are you managing your workload?
5 Are you managing your boss?
6 Are you managing your people?
7 Are you motivating your people?

How good a manager are you?

Before presuming to manage other people, you must first learn to manage yourself. After all, why should your staff accept your suggestions for improving their effectiveness unless you can demonstrate that they work for you too? But this isn't the only reason for seeking to manage yourself better. There's a close link between seeking to manage yourself effectively and developing yourself. Managers have to answer to the organisation that pays their salaries and they have certain responsibilities to colleagues who rely on them. But they are not expected to pursue a policy of selfless altruism. A manager over-burdened with projects no one else will accept, heading up a team of other managers' rejects, and occupying the least desirable office space in the building, may hope for reward in the next life, but they won't achieve much for themselves or their team in this one!

A truly selfless manager would have no scope to change, move or develop, thereby frustrating a vital human requirement: to learn by reviewing past experience in the context of current needs and to make plans for the future which aim to improve the present situation. So selfless managers are stuck – and doomed to fail, along with their teams and perhaps the organisations they work for as well.

Organisations also make different demands on managers in different circumstances. So managers who ignore or misread the current state or climate of their organisation are unlikely to be effective. All management activity is directed towards one of three objectives: survival, maintenance or development. In times of recession, much of a manager's time is devoted to activities designed simply to keep the organisation alive. Planning is almost entirely tactical and short term (there may not be a long term!), with weekly sales figures and manning levels permanently at the top of the agenda.

Maintenance management is designed to sustain an organisation that is not in a life-threatening situation. People need it as much as companies do – keeping physically fit is an obvious analogy. But just as a couch potato will answer the question 'Are you fit?' with the retort 'Fit for what?', so organisations must do more than merely maintain themselves if they are to thrive. In a healthy organisation, the majority of managerial activity is devoted towards development, i.e. aimed to bring about significant change.

Effective managers must be able to perform in all three situations. They also need to understand the links between them. Survival is essential, but only as a means of ensuring that there is something to be maintained. Maintenance is useful, though only as a prelude to development. And while development is the natural state of the healthy organisation, it needs to be punctuated by periods of consolidation (i.e. maintenance) and must never follow a course which puts the organisation's survival at unjustified risk. Finally, you must remember that all three types of management task make demands on three key aspects of yourself: your health (a sound mind in a sound body); your skills (intellectual, technical, personal); and your understanding of yourself (who you are and what you want to become).

The key element in learning to manage yourself is recognising that you can be in control and drive what happens around you. You must believe you have the power to make things happen – for the benefit of yourself and other people. This is the positive view of power – as a tool to liberate people from whatever it is that is stopping them making the most of themselves. Of course, power also has negative connotations – of manipulation or an authoritarian, even dictatorial, approach to management. It can certainly be employed as an instrument of oppression. What distinguishes positive uses from negative abuses is the motivation of the person wielding the power and the ends to which it is being directed. It's one thing to ask other people to respect your rights, but it's a very different thing to deprive them of theirs. Similarly, it is acceptable to put forward your views and pursue your interests with all possible skill and energy. But it is usually counter-productive to try and impose them by railroading, rank-pulling or chicanery.

To be a good people manager, I think you have to excel in four different areas: planning and administration; problem-solving; leadership; and general people management (a catch-all term for a number of different skills that don't fall into any of the other three categories!). Complete the following questionnaire to discover how you compare with other managers. It consists of a description of all the key tasks involved in people management and you will need to rate your own performance on each in turn. Don't spend too long agonising over your judgements. Just give your immediate reaction and remember – good managers don't underestimate or overestimate themselves!

Assess your ability to do the following, by circling one of each line of numbers.

Assessing your managerial skills

	Very good		Average		Poor
Identify higher and lower priority tasks among conflicting job requirements:					
1 *for your own work*	5	④	3	2	1
2 *for the work of your staff*	⑤	4	3	2	1
Organise and readjust work schedules as necessary:					

		Very good		Average		Poor
3	*for your own work*	5	**4**	3	2	1
4	*for the work of your staff*	5	**4**	3	2	1
5	*Remain calm, effective and clear-headed under pressure*	5	4	**3**	2	1
6	*Identify a problem and state it clearly*	5	**4**	3	2	1
7	*Identify the causes of problems and accurately assess their effects*	5	**4**	3	2	1
8	*Bargain with others in order to arrive at solutions that satisfy both parties*	5	4	**3**	2	1
9	*Implement the solutions to problems and monitor the effects*	5	**4**	3	2	1
10	*Recognise useful skills in others and harness them to solve problems*	**5**	4	3	2	1
11	*Work with very little direction*	5	**4**	3	2	1
12	*Demonstrate strong personal commitment to and persistence in achieving goals*	**5**	4	3	2	1
13	*Cope effectively with unexpected problems*	5	**4**	3	2	1
14	*Anticipate problems and make changes before they occur*	5	**4**	3	2	1
15	*Take risks with new ways of doing things*	5	**4**	3	2	1
16	*Use other people's skills by delegating effectively*	**5**	4	3	2	1
17	*Provide regular, personal help, guidance and training to your staff to help them improve their performance*	5	**4**	3	2	1
18	*Establish and communicate clear priorities to your staff*	5	**4**	3	2	1
19	*Consistently give clear-cut decisions to your staff when required*	5	**4**	3	2	1

	Very good		Average		Poor
20 *Regularly review the performance of your staff and frequently provide informal feedback on their performance*	5	4	(3)	2	1
21 *Provide negative feedback constructively*	(5)	4	3	2	1
22 *Recognise good performance rather than just look for problems*	(5)	4	3	2	1
23 *Encourage open exchange of ideas and questions, and encourage discussion of mistakes*	(5)	4	3	2	1
24 *Handle conflict constructively; remain calm and help resolve disagreements*	(5)	4	3	2	1
25 *Identify and attract competent staff to your unit*	5	(4)	3	2	1

How to interpret your scores

Overall scores Add up all the numbers you've circled. If your overall total (i.e. scores on all 25 items) is 100 or above, you appear to be very confident of your management skills. Are you really that good? A score of between 65 and 99 suggests you think you have reasonable management skills, but could improve. What skills need improvement and what are you going to do about it? If you score 64 or less, you feel you have room for a great deal of improvement. But where are you going to start?

Balance of scores Your overall score simply reflects how good a manager you think you are. There is no guarantee that you are right, of course! You may not have much experience of other managers or you may have a blind spot when it comes to judging your own performance. A more useful measure is the balance of your scores on the four different components (planning/administration; problem-solving; leadership; people management).

Calculate a sub-score for each of them as follows:

1 add up your scores on items 1–5 to gain a *planning/administration* sub-total; 2 1

2 add up your scores on items 6–10 to get your *problem-solving* skills sub-total;

3 to calculate your *leadership* skills sub-total, simply add up your scores on items 11–15;

4 to calculate your *people management* skills sub-total, add up your scores on items 16–25 on the questionnaire and divide the sum by two.

Inspect the sub-totals to work out which – in your estimation – are your personal strong and weak points. See if your line manager and the members of your team agree with your results. Point out to them that these are your judgements of your own performance, not those of an outsider, and that they are subjective rather than objective. Ask them to judge you in general and specific terms, and brace yourself for one or two disappointments! You may, however, be pleasantly surprised to find that they rate you more highly than you rate yourself in at least some respects.

Once you have agreed on the areas in which you need to improve your performance, you may wish to try the following management development exercise. Think of a real-life situation which occurred in the last three months when you were particularly successful in achieving a task connected with each of the four major categories identified above (i.e. planning and administration, problem-solving, leadership and people management). Tackle one at a time by writing a brief description of: the situation, the key factors contributing to your success, and lessons learnt from the experience. Then think of a situation in the same area of management in which you did not achieve your objective. Write a brief description of the situation, what went wrong, the actions you took to resolve the setback, and the lessons you learnt from it.

These exercises will give you an idea of your main strengths and weaknesses as a people manager, and the basis of a remedial action programme to raise your game. And yet, if you are like most managers, you will probably still have a feeling that you could be so much more effective, *if only* . . .

Here are some of the most common excuses managers give for falling short of their ideals, together with suggestions for shifting your thinking.

The 'if only' syndrome

EXCUSES	REMEDIES
If only . . .	

I had more time/less to do

Time is something you create for yourself; your workload is a collection of tasks you accepted. Better planning, more delegation, the courage to say 'No' – and less whingeing, please!

my staff listened to me

Nobody has to listen. It's the communicator's job to command attention. Better preparation, clearer presentation, more careful choice of time and tone – make it worth their while listening to you.

they let me run things my way

They'd probably love to, if you showed them you were willing to be responsible and truly accountable for your operation. You need to earn their trust and ask for power. Find out why they haven't given it to you before.

we didn't have so many conflicting interests

Conflict is inevitable and ought to be useful in an organisation of any size. Different functions have different objectives, but there's no need for clashes to become personal. Concentrate on solving your own immediate problems rather than trying to reshape the organisation.

I didn't have my boss on my back all the time

Chances are he or she would much rather be somewhere else, too. Reassure them you don't need constant attention and point out that you could do a much better job for them if they allowed you to get on with it.

I didn't have so many interruptions

Chance would be a fine thing! In a busy office, it's just not possible to insist on complete isolation. However, people recognise that certain tasks have absolute priority and they will respect requests for temporary freedom from interruption – but don't overdo it.

EXCUSES	REMEDIES

If only . . .

there wasn't so much paperwork

Everyone in organisations believes they are either swamped with paperwork or kept in the dark. The former is by far the lesser of two evils. You don't have to read all the paper that appears on your desk and a simple colour coding system for communications can make life much easier.

they weren't always moving the goal posts

Give thanks that they do! In a changing environment, it's essential to monitor what's happening and adjust strategy to meet new requirements. Fixed goalposts indicate a closed corporate mind – and a short, undignified descent into oblivion.

I could see light at the end of the tunnel

Effective managers need patience, vision that extends beyond the end of their nose, and a steady nerve. They also require resolution in the face of disappointment, belief in the direction in which the organisation is heading and the ability to motivate themselves.

people took me more seriously

But how seriously do you take yourself? Self-deprecation can easily be mistaken for self-doubt. Work without humour would be intolerable, but MBFA (management by fooling around) is no substitute for the real thing.

they told me what was going on

They probably do, if you read/listened to what was sent/said to you. And if they don't, it's your responsibility to point out deficiencies in the internal communications system. It's also possible that your complaints about paperwork (see above) are being taken at face value.

the boss let me know that my contribution is valued

You may have a point here. Praise, recognition and acknowledgement are conspicuous by their absence in the traditional management development curriculum. You can always ask

	for feedback, however, and if your immediate superior has a block about providing it, you may be able to obtain it from another source.
I could trust my staff to do more	You could, you could – *if only* you trusted yourself! You selected them, you should have trained them, and it's entirely up to you what you delegate and how you do it.

Most managers find that the *if only* exercise speaks for itself. Even the best managers have their areas of weakness. In fact, it's usually the best ones who are most willing to identify their weaknesses and the first to take steps to remedy them.

What do good managers do?

At the most general level, successful managers tend to have four characteristics:

- they take enormous pleasure and pride in the growth of their people;

- they are basically cheerful optimists – someone has to keep up morale when setbacks occur;

- they don't promise more than they can deliver;

- when they move on from a job, they always leave the situation a little better than it was when they arrived.

More specifically, here is a list of the essential tasks at which a manager must excel if he or she is to be truly effective.

Good managers

- *Select and retain good staff*   There can be no hiding behind such expressions as 'You just can't get the staff these days'. There are always good people around. Your job is to make sure that they come and work with you! Having got them, however – by whatever means – you must then keep them. This involves creating an environment which good people simply don't want to leave. The way to do so is to follow the criteria set out below.

● *Keep them well informed*   Effective communication is essential. People, especially good people, want to know what's going on around them – how the team is doing, where it's headed and, above all, where they fit into the scheme of things.

● *Help them improve*   Other things being equal, people prefer to do a good job rather than a bad one. But they also never lose interest in doing the job better. It may not be possible to provide people with variety by changing their jobs. But it's always possible to look for new ways of carrying out the same task more effectively, which may be enough to keep them interested.

● *Know how to negotiate*   By negotiation I mean dealing with people in the broadest sense, not simply in an industrial/pay-bargaining situation. You have to reach understandings with people from the moment you wake up in the morning until the end of the day. In fact, by the time you reach your desk, you may well have completed negotiations with half a dozen people – your partner, the children, a traffic warden, the doorman, a colleague you met in the corridor on the way in etc.

● *Handle conflict constructively*   In all lively teams, conflict is inevitable. Talented people will always have views of their own, and there is no point in hiring people for the quality of their thinking and then trying to suppress it, or simply bringing them round to your way of thought! Conflicts must be brought out into the open and debated, and it is the manager's job to see that people who lose the argument do not lose face or their enthusiasm.

● *Make decisions*   Some people believe that there is no such thing as a good or a bad decision, only decisions! Their thinking is that problems can often be tackled in a number of different ways, equally effectively. They cannot, however, be solved until a decision is made about what particular course of action is going to be followed. Certainly, managers who have a reputation for indecisiveness rarely attract or keep the best people.

● *Plan and prioritise*　To have any chance of succeeding as a manager, you have to look ahead and you have to make decisions about the order in which you are going to do things. The reason for both is the same: you have a very great deal to do!

● *Delegate effectively*　Managers who refuse to delegate, or who do so in a way that guarantees that the person to whom the work is delegated is almost bound to fail, rarely attract the best staff. You must delegate rather than abdicate, i.e. you do not lose interest in or responsibility for work that you pass on to others, and you think carefully about what is to be delegated and to whom. You do not simply distribute the tedious aspects of your job to anyone who doesn't look particularly busy. You must also realise that delegation should benefit both yourself and your people. You are released for other, higher-level work, and they receive an opportunity to develop themselves.

● *Function under pressure*　Not even the most effective manager can ever create a situation which is literally pressure-free. Good managers certainly reduce the impact of pressure, and minimise its sources, but the business environment is too complex and unpredictable for it to be realistic to aim to eliminate pressure altogether. To be successful, therefore, you must be a pressure player. Not a pressure junkie – one of those people who creates problems for themselves when things seem to be going too easily – or a fire-fighter (which usually means a fire-raiser!), but someone who is not thrown off balance by pressure, and regards stress as a stimulant rather than a signal to panic.

● *Solve and learn from problems*　Working life inevitably has its share of problems, and it is an important part of the manager's job not to solve all of them, but to have created a situation in which they can and will be solved by those most competent to do so. It is all too easy to allow problems to grind you down. The effective manager must create a completely different response to them. The first task must always be to solve them and bring to an end whatever situation the problem has caused. But you should then seek to avenge yourself on the problem for the irritation or damage it has caused! We shall see how to do this in Chapter 4.

● *Lead by example* Giving clear messages lies at the very heart of effective management. 'Do what I say, not what I do!' is a classic mixed message, and exactly the sort of thing that causes good people to leave a team. You need credibility and consistency if you are to be an effective leader. You need only look at the outrage caused by senior managers who take large pay rises for themselves while urging their subordinates to show restraint, to understand how demotivating it can be when the boss is clearly operating the principle of 'one law for the rich, another for the poor'.

● *Take calculated risks* Managers have to take decisions about the future, but unfortunately they do not have a crystal ball! It is not given to any of us to be able to forecast accurately what is actually going to happen, which means that there must inevitably be an element of risk in most decision-making. The secret is to accept this and to take all possible steps to reduce the downside of whatever course of action you have decided upon. We saw earlier that taking no risks is probably the riskiest option of all in a changing environment. Therefore taking a carefully calculated risk is probably the least dangerous path you can follow.

● *Encourage new ways of doing things* One of the most vital duties a manager has is to be the person who acquires new skills, thinking and attitudes. How and where you do so is your business. But once you have taken on board anything new and important, your first action must be to pass it on to at least one other member of your team. You must also play the role of cheerleader for anyone who is trying out something new. You should actively encourage suggestions for new ways of doing things, on the basis that no one knows more about a job and hence about ways of improving it, than the person who is carrying it out. What usually inhibits people from trying new ways of doing things is the fear of failure. It is the manager's job to create an atmosphere in which failure is perfectly acceptable when something new is being tried, provided that it is a sensible thing to try and that it's carried out in a sensible fashion, i.e. in a way that gives it a reasonable chance of success.

These are the essential tasks that every good manager must master. But what about the *great* manager? I was recently asked what I thought were the 10 characteristics displayed by the very best managers I have ever encountered. After some thought, I came up with this list.

Great managers

- *Accept blame*   When the big wheel from head office visits the site and expresses displeasure, the great manager immediately accepts full responsibility. In everyday working life, the best managers are constantly aware that they selected and should have developed their people. So any errors made by team members are in a very real sense their responsibility.

- *Give praise*   Praise is probably the most under-used management tool. Great managers are forever trying to catch their people doing something right, and congratulating them on it. And when praise comes from outside, they are swift not merely to publicise the fact, but to make clear who has earned it. Managers who regularly give praise are in a much stronger position to criticise or reprimand poor performance. If you simply comment when you are dissatisfied with performance, it is all too common for your words to be taken as a straightforward expression of personal dislike. 'I don't like the way you are doing that', is all too easily heard as 'I don't like you'. The way around this is simple. A great manager never criticises without congratulating the person being criticised on some aspect of their performance. 'I didn't like the way you did that, and what made it particularly surprising is that you did it so well last week.'

- *Make blue sky*   Very few people are comfortable with the idea that they will be doing exactly what they are doing today in 10 years' time. Great managers try to be ahead of the game in this respect. They anticipate people's dissatisfaction and think of ways to deal with boredom before it becomes a problem. Managers are usually better placed than their people to see the range of career opportunities open to them, so great managers are constantly reviewing the situation to work out what is best for their people in the future. In large organisations, blue sky is usually visible upwards, via promotion. But it may also be found to the side, by a switch of function or department. Sometimes, particularly in very small organisations, the only way to achieve blue sky is by introducing a new way of doing a familiar task. Great managers accept that sometimes they will have to tell good people that they can't see any way of catering for their ambitions and therefore advise them – and actively help them – to find a position elsewhere.

- *Listen before and after talking*   Good communicators always check that their words have been heard and are being acted upon. Great communicators, however, are those who realise that you must start listening before planning the communication. You need to approach your target audience and find out where they stand on the critical issues so that you can tailor-make a presentation to anticipate likely objections and press all the right buttons (there will be more of this in Chapter 5).

- *Let go*   This refers not merely to the delegation of tasks, but also to releasing other more subtle reins: for example, responsibility for setting the tone of a team or changing the corporate sub-culture.

- *Put themselves about*   Most managers now accept the need to get out and about to find out not merely what their team is thinking, but what the rest of the world, including their customers, is saying. So MBWA (management by walking about) is an excellent thing, though it has to be distinguished from MBWAWP (management by walking about – without purpose!), where senior management wander around aimlessly, annoying customers, worrying staff, breaking things and generally making a nuisance of themselves.

- *Judge on merit*   This is a great deal more difficult than it sounds. It's virtually impossible to divorce your feelings about someone – whether you like or dislike them – from how you view their actions. The tendency is to notice only the good things about people we approve of, and the bad things about those we are less keen on. But suspicions of discrimination or favouritism are fatal to the smooth running of any team, so the great manager accepts this as an aspect of the game that really needs to be worked on.

- *Exploit strengths, not weaknesses – in themselves and in their people*   Weak managers feel threatened by other people's strengths. It's not uncommon to observe them moving people out of jobs they are actually doing too well – the fear presumably being that the manager's job is at risk. Weak managers also revel in the discovery of weakness, and regard it as something to be exploited rather than remedied. Great managers have no truck with this negative, destructive thinking. They see strengths, in themselves as well as in other people, as things to be built on, and weakness as something to be accommodated, worked around and, if possible, eliminated.

- *Make things happen, rather than preventing them*   The old-fashioned approach to management was rather like the old-fashioned approach to child-rearing, 'Go and see what the children are doing and tell them to stop it!'. Great managers have confidence that their people will be working in their interests, and therefore do everything they can to create an environment in which people feel free to express themselves and act. The Gestapo approach to management, favoured by old-fashioned personnel departments, is totally inimical to creative thinking or the smooth running of an effective team.

● *Make themselves redundant*   This is not as drastic as it sounds! What great managers do is learn new skills and acquire useful information from the outside world, and then immediately pass them on, to ensure that if they were to be run down by a bus, the team would still have the benefit of the new information. It is a sound principle that no one in an organisation should be doing work that could be accomplished equally effectively by someone less well paid than themselves. So great managers are perpetually on the look-out for higher-level activities to occupy their own time, while constantly passing on tasks that they have already mastered. This has the additional benefit of preventing them from becoming stale.

Why is it difficult to be a good manager?

Reading through the attributes of good and great managers, and still feeling a warm glow of achievement after having completed the management skills questionnaire, you may be wondering why so many managers consider the task to be a difficult one. I think there are two main sets of reasons, the first being that managers face at least four groups of conflicting demands.

The first is Management versus Administration. You want to be giving your attention to the important parts of the management role detailed above, but find yourself submerged under a sea of administrative detail.

The second conflict is Effectiveness versus Efficiency of the operation you are trying to manage. The danger here is of becoming so obsessed with the way things are done, and the extent to which procedures are being followed, that you lose sight of whether or not your objectives are being met. In other words, your focus is all on input and method, rather than output and outcome. Of course it's important to observe the way that things are done, but this should never be allowed to override actual achievements and accomplishments.

The third conflict which managers have to resolve is Overseeing versus Doing. It's very difficult to watch someone perform a task less effectively than you could do it yourself. You use the justification that you can't bear watching them fail. But this is exactly what you have to do, if they are ever to become as competent at it as you are.

The final conflict that many managers find hampers them, is Innovating versus Adapting. Experts are forever telling us that we should be searching constantly for new ways of doing things. In the real world, however, the show must go on. You can't call operations to a halt while the team re-equips itself, or submits to a structural overhaul, or devises a totally new way of doing things. Most managers have to resort to Management by Sellotape in order to keep things together. There is, after all, no point in designing a wonderful new way of running your business if you have no business left to run!

I think these conflicts are an inevitable part of the management task. However, they aren't the only reason why management is difficult. Unfortunately, many managers contribute to their own discomfort. In addition to the 'If onlys' we looked at earlier, there are a number of attitudes managers choose to adopt which make their task more difficult. Here are six of these attitudes, expressed in statements.

● *'I must do something because that's what a manager is employed for'* This is simply not true. Managers are supposed to make things happen, not necessarily do them themselves. In some circumstances, action may be exactly what is *not* called for.

● *'I've seen this one before'* The problem here is one of over-familiarity. You've probably seen it in the behaviour of a doctor, faced with a crowded surgery in the middle of an epidemic. They're already writing out a prescription before the patient in front of them has even started talking, so certain are they that they know what the problem is. At work, this type of attitude is especially dangerous because it leads a manager to ignore the vital contribution that new members of the team have to make. Very often, their inexperience makes them ideally suited to produce a creative new solution to a problem that has never been properly solved before.

● *'Without all the facts, I can't possibly make a decision'* In the real world, alas, having all the facts is a rare luxury. Of course it's wise to postpone a decision as long as you safely can, while new relevant information is still coming in. But effective managers know that the timing of the decision is rarely within their control – and almost never driven by the consideration that all the facts are now in.

● *'I must solve my subordinates' problems for them'* This is not the task of the manager. What you are supposed to do is enable your subordinates to solve their own problems, by pointing them in the right direction, i.e. towards the right people and material to help them find solutions. By solving their problems for them, you are holding back their development and preventing them from fulfilling their potential.

● *'This problem is so important, it must be solved immediately'* Again, this is almost the opposite of the truth. The more important the problem, the more urgent it is that the decision made should be the right one. Only trivial decisions should be made fast!

● *'My door is always open'* Managers tend to utter these words with great pride. They genuinely believe that this is the cry of the concerned, humane boss. It's not. What it displays is an inability to get inside other people's heads. After all, how likely is it that a junior member of staff is going to come into your office, where they can see all the trappings of your position, and say anything revealing? If you take the trouble to go to visit them where they feel most at ease, which will probably be at their workplace, there is just a chance that they may trust you enough to open up. But the boss's office is surely the last place where you can expect true frankness – however great a manager you are!

Are you managing your workload?

The key to effective management – of yourself and of others – is the ability to manage your resources within the constraints of time, budgets, the market, your boss and the political environment. Time is probably the most important 'If only' and the first thing to appreciate is that if you find yourself saying 'I just don't have enough time', then it is probably your own fault.

It's all too easy to blame everybody else for the fact that you have to take work home, that you miss deadlines, that the day's work is never planned, that you end up doing everything yourself because nobody else can do it and that you never have time to prepare for all those meetings. You can convince yourself that the reason other people cope better than you is because your job is different or more demanding, and your staff cannot give you adequate support. The reality is that every job has its tensions and stresses. Getting control of your time is your responsibility and the problem belongs to nobody but you.

There are various stages of attempting to manage your time. The first stage is analysis – finding out where there is scope for improving the use of your time.

Start with your job – the tasks you have to carry out and the objectives you are there to achieve. Try to establish an order of priority between your tasks and objectives. I know it's not easy, particularly if you have a number of conflicting areas of responsibility, but here is a simple system which may help. You classify all tasks that face you according to their urgency and their importance, place them in the appropriate box and follow the course of action recommended in it.

Course of Action

Urgent	**DO IT!**	**Delegate It**
Not Urgent	**Plan It**	**Leave It**
Classification	*Important*	*Not Important*

Having sorted out your priorities, you should analyse in more detail how you spend your time. This will identify the time-consuming activities and indicate where there are problems, as well as solutions to them. The best way to do this is to keep a diary. Do this for a week or two, dividing the day into 15-minute sections and noting down what you did in each period. Against each space, summarise how effectively you spent your time by writing 'V' for valuable, 'D' for doubtful, and 'U' for useless. At the end of each week, analyse your time under either the following headings or relevant headings for your work: reading, writing, dictating, telephoning, dealing with people, attending meetings, travelling, other.

Then, analyse the ratings under each heading. This will give you the information you need to spot any weaknesses in your time management. Identify and bring under control the areas in which your time tends to slip away unprofitably. Research shows that the most common time-stealers are:

- confused responsibility and authority

- a lack of objectives and priorities

- ineffective delegation

- meetings

- telephone interruptions

- visitors who drop in

- emergencies

- trying to do too much at once

- cluttered desk/personal disorganisation

- indecision/procrastination

- an inability to say 'No'

- unclear communication

- delayed or inaccurate information

- tasks left unfinished

- untrained or inadequate staff.

Try to plan ahead as much as possible. Use your diary – attempt to have at least one day a week free of meetings and avoid filling any day with appointments. This will leave blocks of unallocated time for planning, thinking, reading, writing and dealing with the unexpected.

There are two ways in which diaries can be used to help you organise your time. The first is as a *weekly organiser*. Sit down at the beginning of each week with your diary and plan how you are going to spend your time. Assess each of your projects or tasks and work out your priorities. Leave blocks of time for dealing with correspondence and seeing people. Try to preserve one free day or at least half a day if it is at all possible.

You should also use your diary as a *daily organiser*. At the beginning of each day, consult your diary to check on your plans and commitments. Refer to the previous day's organiser to find out what is still outstanding. Inspect your pending tray and in-tray to check what remains and what has just arrived, then write down the things to do: meetings or interviews; telephone calls; tasks in order of priority.

Identify what must be done today, what should ideally be done today but could be left until tomorrow, and what can be dealt with later. Plan broadly when you are going to do your first two priority tasks. Tick off your tasks as they are completed, retaining the list in order to consult it the following day.

Such devices are only one aid to more effective time planning. Other people can also help, providing you ask, guide and encourage them. Effective time management relies to a great extent on delegation of work tasks. Many managers are scared of losing control and refuse to give away any of their precious workload, although this inevitably means they are overworked. Others don't have time to do their own job properly, because they are also trying to do half a dozen other people's jobs for them. To understand how this bizarre state of affairs arises, I need to introduce you to one of the most vivid images of management practice – the Monkey.

Picture yourself hurrying along a corridor, briefcase under your arm, hands full of papers, on your way to an important meeting. In front of you looms the person you least want to see – your most demanding subordinate, with a look on his face that tells you he wants help. Without pausing to draw breath, you snatch the sheet of paper he's holding and say: 'Can't stop now. Leave it with me. I'll give you a call after lunch.' What you have just done to get him off your back is ludicrous. Not only have you agreed to do someone else's job, you have even agreed to give him a progress report – all without being asked. It's the classic mistake of the manager who needs to be loved and doesn't realise that they're doing their people a disservice by not allowing them to find a solution to their own problems. The Monkey symbolises a Problem. In this instance, your subordinate is its proper keeper, charged with housing and feeding it. The moment you grabbed the offending sheet of paper, there was a flurry of fur as the Monkey leapt from his shoulder to yours. You need to check the area around your neck pretty regularly, to make sure it hasn't become a haven for errant apes.

Are you managing your boss?

Other things being equal, the most significant relationship you have at work is likely to be the one with your boss. She or he can be your most important ally, your most ardent champion and your most useful critic. Your boss can also ruin your career, your marriage and even threaten your life. So it's worth devoting a little time to thinking about the art of handling bosses.

It all starts with understanding what they say. Here's a selective dictionary of 'Boss-Speak'. See how good you are at translating what they say into what they mean.

WHAT BOSSES SAY	WHAT THEY REALLY MEAN
'Thank you for your contribution'	'You've said enough for now, so shut up!'
'Can you shed any light on this?'	'I want you to get me out of this mess'
'What's your workload like now?'	'I'm going to pile this lot on you, whether you like it or not'
'We need a meeting about this'	'I need some ideas, and fast'
'I know you'll make the decision'	'I don't know what I'm talking about here, so you'd better handle it'

WHAT BOSSES SAY	WHAT THEY REALLY MEAN
'I know you're the only person who can handle this'	'There's a disgruntled client on the telephone, and I can't be bothered to deal with him'
'I don't mean to be critical'	'I *do* mean to be critical'
'This is rather a grey area'	'I'm clueless'
'Just one tiny thing before you go'	'Hope you don't mind missing *EastEnders*/ getting a later train/ cancelling your date . . .'

Not all misunderstandings with the boss can be put down to their double-talk. Often we are our own worst enemies, because we mysteriously lose the ability to articulate the one word that could fight off so many work problems. That word is 'No!'. Learning to refuse politely but convincingly is a key management skill. But it rests on having the confidence to recognise and defend your legitimate rights, i.e. to behave assertively. Here is an exercise to discover how assertive you are. Answer all the questions 'Yes' or 'No'.

		YES	NO
1	*Do you find it difficult to say no to any kind of demand made on you?*	☐	☐
2	*If someone went to the front of the queue, would you do something about it?*	☑	☐
3	*Do you usually put yourself second in family matters?*	☑	☐
4	*Do you believe that you must fight for your rights, or risk losing them altogether?*	☑	☑
5	*Do you make a point of complaining if you are sold shoddy goods?*	☑	☐
6	*Do you have great difficulty in leaving situations when you have had enough?*	☐	☑
7	*Do you find it difficult to get rid of a sales person who is persistent and wasting your time?*	☐	☑
8	*Do you hesitate about asking a stranger directions in the street?*	☐	☑

		YES	NO
9	*If you were working on a committee, would you tend to take charge of things?*	☐	☑
10	*If you have been given poor service in a restaurant or hotel, do you always make a fuss?*	☑	☐

Score two points for each 'Yes' answer to questions 2, 4, 5, 9 and 10, and zero for every 'No'. For each 'No' answer to questions 1, 3, 6, 7 and 8, score two points, and zero for each 'Yes'. The higher your score, the more assertive you are. A score of 14 or more suggests that you have what is sometimes called a strong personality. You insist on other people respecting your rights, and may even be seen as pushy. Between 9 and 13 points means that you know your rights, but only make demands if it is an important matter. A score of 8 or less indicates that you are submissive – a follower rather than a leader – and may be regarded as a pushover.

I'm not suggesting that the effective manager's only ambition should be to impress the boss. But you will get more done if he or she is on your side. You need to make them trust you, rely on you, and believe in your ability to come up with good ideas and make things happen. Here are a few general principles to help achieve your goal.

- *Help your boss to be right* – and respond quickly to requests on a 'can do, will do' basis.

- *Don't give your boss nasty surprises* – the kinds that prompt the response, 'You should have told me about this before!'.

- *Don't cover up problems until it becomes too late for careful thought and action* – talk about them in good time, so that fire-fighting isn't the only solution.

- *Prepare the ground for decision-making* – don't present your boss with the need for an immediate answer.

- *Don't just think about your own position, consider the total business context* – avoid special pleading and be prepared to make concessions.

- *Don't send your boss copies of your work to show how clever you have been* – turn to your colleagues for instant gratification.

- *Prepare your case fully before you meet the boss* – give alternatives and impartial advice.

- *Seek advice only on complex problems and supply details in advance* – don't expect the boss to absorb difficult issues and come up with instant answers.

- *The boss's decision is final – once made, it must be carried out as if it were yours* – of course you should press your view initially, but in the end you must give way even if you don't agree.

- *Be positive!* – offer solutions, take initiatives. Whining is depressing and unwelcome.

- *Be brief* – you are only one problem in the boss's day of problems.

Not every boss is trustworthy, supportive or even competent. Even in a perfect world, the relationship between superior and subordinate still wouldn't be free of problems. However, these guidelines should make your upwards communications a little easier.

Are you managing your people?

Effective managers begin the task of people management at the beginning. They insist on choosing the people they are to manage. Despite a wealth of evidence showing how unreliable they are as a means of selection, interviews remain by far the most commonly used method. An increasing number of organisations, recognising the damage that can be done by employing the wrong people, are experimenting with alternative methods, such as Assessment Centres. But for the foreseeable future, most managers will be relying on interviews, so it is as well to be aware of their pitfalls and of ways to improve your interviewing technique.

Never rely on your judgement alone. Interviewing works best as a series of one-to-one meetings, with the different interviewers only coming together to discuss a candidate at the end of the process. You should avoid panel interviews and any other techniques designed to augment the stress inevitably associated with the situation. You may be concerned with how people respond under pressure, but you ought to be more interested in what they are capable of when they are at their best. You must prepare a structure for each interview, and the main thrust of your investigation should be track record, since this is the most reliable index of future performance. Don't accept everything you are told. Check everything you can, for example by taking up references and, ideally, actually speaking to referees. Avoid cloning; the fact that someone is very like you should be a reason for *not* employing them, rather than the reverse. If you possibly can, try and create a situation in which they are actually performing the job you are considering them for, or carrying out a simulation of important aspects of the work.

New people need to be welcomed on board properly. First impressions are crucial, and they may never recover from the impact of the wrong sort of introduction. They must be given a chance to meet everyone and to discuss with you exactly what you expect of them. They will, of course, be given a proper job description. But you should also make it clear that once they have had time to get their feet under the desk, you'll be interested to hear their suggestions as to how the job could be done better. If you're serious about empowering people and helping them develop, and truly responsive to the importance of individual differences, how better to demonstrate your commitment than by offering newcomers the opportunity to redesign their own jobs? It will reduce stress and boredom, and minimise any risk of resentment and unexploited brainpower.

The more successfully a new member is integrated into the team, the greater the risk that you will simply leave them to it, congratulating yourself on a job well done, and then turn your attention towards problems. This is, of course, the perfect way to undo your good work and add to your list of problems. Even the best, most experienced staff will always need help in the form of appraisal, assessment of their training and development needs, and career planning.

You should aim to have regular, structured and – ideally – two-way formal appraisal sessions with *all* your people, however senior. These must be supported by ongoing coaching, where necessary, and a commitment to arrange for access to counselling if this is required. Coaching is different from training in that it is one to one, occurs on the job, works from where the person being coached actually is rather than where they ought to be, builds on personal strengths, aims to remedy weaknesses and involves constant feedback. All feedback should be:

- specific ('I didn't like the way you dealt with that customer'), not general ('I don't like your attitude');

- descriptive ('When you said that, I felt ignored'), not evaluative ('Only a monster could be so insensitive!');

- realistic ('Why not make a list of what's going wrong?'), not impossible ('What you need is a brain transplant!').

Feedback should also be clearly for the benefit of the person being coached, not an ego trip for the person delivering it. Effective feedback is balanced between constructive criticism and deserved praise. Of course, there's another sort of criticism, designed solely to censure and knock down, without any thought of building up. Feedback and censure differ, in tone and in outcome, as you can see from the following descriptions.

FEEDBACK IS:	CENSURE IS:
information designed to change behaviour in a positive way	dumping my anger – telling you how you should be
specific	general
descriptive	evaluative
tough on issues	tough on person
clear	fuzzy
future-oriented	past-oriented
intended to find solutions	intended to attribute blame

Appraisal and coaching sessions have a useful spin-off: they help identify individual training and development needs. These tend to change more quickly than you anticipate, so it's important to monitor them regularly. Where training programmes are concerned, research shows that their long-term effectiveness depends at least as much on the effort put into their preparation and follow-up, as it does on the delivery of the actual training message. So managers are implicated in the outcome of all the training their people receive, regardless of whether or not they carry out or attend a particular session. Trainers tell delegates that what they get out of a session is determined largely by how much they put into it. But it's also crucially affected by the frame of mind in which they approach the session and the thoroughness with which their performance is monitored afterwards – both managerial responsibilities.

Are you motivating your people?

Motivation is arguably the manager's most important area of responsibility. Think about your people. Do any of them display any of the following classic symptoms of the demotivated worker?

- Apathy and indifference to the job.

- Poor timekeeping, high absenteeism.

- Exaggeration of problems, disputes and grievances.

- Refusal to stand in for colleagues.

- Unwillingness to accommodate change (why bother, when you're not going to be around to see it?).

Or do they perhaps seem to you to bear all the hallmarks of the contented worker?

- High performance, results consistently achieved.

- Energy, enthusiasm, determination to succeed.

- Unstinting co-operation in overcoming problems.

- Willingness to accept responsibility.

- Willingness to accommodate change.

Beware of painting too rosy a picture, though. How well do you really know your people and what turns them on? Here's an exercise to test your knowledge of human nature, and a chance to discover whether you've really shaken off the old Them and Us mentality that used to bedevil British managers.

Inspect the following list of things that different people look for in their job. Your task is to rank them in order of importance (1 for most important, 8 for least) for yourself (using the boxes in the left-hand column) and for the most junior member of your team (using the boxes in the right-hand column).

	WHAT DO YOU WANT?		WHAT DO YOU THINK THEY WANT?
□ 8	good working conditions	□
□ 7	support/loyalty of boss	□
□ 6	interesting work	□
□ 3	high salary	□
□ 1	job security	□
□ 5	feeling of being involved/ knowing what is going on	□
□ 4	full appreciation of work done	□
□ 2	opportunities for promotion	□

Ask your junior colleague to do the same, this time giving their real preferences and trying to guess yours. If the results surprise you, you're in good company. We have used this exercise in a great many organisations and a consistent pattern emerges. The tendency is for managers to assume that their subordinates (and workers in general) are mainly interested in the basics, while they have their minds fixed firmly on higher things. Staff take precisely the opposite view: it is they who are the disinterested idealists, while their managers are the money-grabbers. Here is a typical example of how workers feel about themselves and their managers.

	WORKERS ON MANAGERS	WORKERS ON THEMSELVES
High salary	1	4
Job security	2	3
Opportunities for promotion	3	6
Good working conditions	4	8
Interesting work	5	5
Support/loyalty from manager	6	7
Full appreciation of work done	7	1
Feeling of being involved/knowing what is going on	8	2

Motivators fall into two categories: *extrinsic* (cash, holidays, material goodies, working conditions) and *intrinsic* (a friendly company, a sense of purpose and achievement, the feeling that you know what's going on and that you're competent at your job). It's the intrinsic, more psychological factors that people cite when they are asked what they enjoy about their job, but the extrinsic that they focus on when they are asked why they left a job. So, job satisfaction isn't a simple mirror image of dissatisfaction.

Different folks do require different strokes and it's a crucial management skill to be able to work out quickly and accurately what's going to work with a new member of your team. As a simple rule of thumb, extroverts respond better to praise, while introverts are more influenced by censure. The stick may be an effective weapon in the short term, but it loses value in the longer term because it increases staff turnover. On the other hand, managers who are only capable of giving good news will find their task becomes very uncomfortable when the going gets rough.

Certain principles of motivation are so powerful that they override personality differences. Here are some of the most important of them.

● *The link between reward and effort* Rewards are much more effective if people know what they are going to get when they work hard and effectively. But the link has to be set up in advance, with expectations and targets agreed. The good motivator/manager makes a point of acknowledging

achievements and uses praise lavishly when it has been
earned – but only when it has been earned, since praising
merely to create a pleasant atmosphere cheapens the
currency.

● *Control and competence*   The feeling of being good at
your job and being in control of your immediate working
environment is the perfect recipe for job satisfaction and
optimum work performance. Conversely, having too much to
do, being stretched beyond your competence, or not really
understanding exactly what is expected of you is a formula for
demotivation. Your people must believe that what they do or
don't achieve is largely determined by them. The feeling that
they are at the mercy of events or have an unpredictable boss
is an instant turn-off and a sure-fire way of getting your
people to turn their attention to the Appointments Vacant
pages.

● *Communication and involvement*   These factors are
discussed extensively elsewhere in the book. Their role in
the motivation equation is dramatically illustrated by the
results of employee attitude surveys. They show that you
can't expect anyone to work well if they don't know what's
expected of them or why they're being asked to do it. And
the only way to get sustained effort out of people who derive
no direct financial benefit from the organisation's success is to
wage a continual 'hearts and minds' campaign to convince
them that their work is important to the organisation and that
they are important to you. Almost the first principle to grasp
about motivation is that the only person you can motivate
directly is yourself. Where other people are concerned, all
you can do is create an atmosphere in which they choose
to motivate themselves. It is a crucial part of the manager's
task to create this atmosphere and you can only do it by
communicating effectively (more on communication skills in
Chapter 5).

Given the importance of effective motivation, here is a list to remind you of some of the things a manager can do to create and sustain the right atmosphere. You should:

- ensure that the relationship between effort and reward is clearly defined;

- set targets and standards which are achievable – but not too easily;

- let people know where they stand;

- recognise achievements, but not cheapen praise;

- make it clear that what people achieve or fail to achieve is up to them;

- increase individuals' responsibility by delegating more;

- allow people maximum scope to vary the methods, sequence and pace of their work;

- remove as many controls as possible while making sure that everyone knows who is responsible for achieving defined targets or meeting standards;

- get more people involved in planning work and innovating;

- make sure that staff are fully informed about decisions that are going to affect them and are kept up to date about everything that is going on in the company;

- allocate work in such a way that everyone has a chance to take on more responsibility and gain more expertise.

The most effective motivators are not always the best liked – in the short term. In the long term, however, most people would rather hear the truth from their manager, even if it is unwelcome. And if you want to know whether you're an effective motivator, why not ask your people? Not that you'll really need to. The results should speak for themselves.

Chapter 3

Huddling up

If the first three rules of good management are 'know yourself', 'manage yourself' and 'motivate others', then the fourth must surely relate to the group of people you work with – your team. The word 'team' conjures up images of groups of people playing or working together, pulling in the same direction, enjoying camaraderie and the sense of shared purpose or a common goal. In sport, the goal is to enjoy the game and defeat the opponent, through the team's concerted effort. The fuel for this effort is provided by each player's motivation. They are willing members of the team, each with a position to fill and a role to play. And they are hungry for success.

Of course, genuine teamwork takes time to develop. The fact is that teams don't work automatically. Sometimes a collection of talented specialists fails to gel – as many football managers have found to their cost. Teamwork needs to be nurtured and it can break down for any one of a host of reasons. So we'll need to keep a look-out for ways of rating team performance. First, though, have a look at the following questions which will focus your mind on the tasks of building, maintaining and working in teams.

1   What is teamwork and why is it important?
2   What's the difference between a group and a team?
3   What are the key indicators of a successful team?
4   What are the symptoms of poor teamwork?
5   How should you pick your team?
6   How important is the leader?
7   Why bother with meetings?
8   How can you tell whether your team is motivated?

Take a look at your professional and personal life. Do you belong to any teams? You may subscribe to a professional body, or belong to a special project group at work, a social club, a PTA, a holiday club, a sports team, an evening class, a charity group – the possibilities are almost endless! Make a list of the teams you belong to. Of course they come in many different shapes and sizes. You could be part of a group of 3, 20 or even a fluctuating membership. In one, you may be the linchpin; in another just part of the silent minority. We saw in Chapter 1 how many different roles people play at work. As you shift roles, you're probably moving from one team to another, often without realising it. Teams can be formal or informal, large or small, long term or short term, with specific or general functions, and with members from diverse or similar backgrounds.

Look at your list and pick the three teams which are most important to you. Don't limit your choice to work. Write their names on separate pieces of paper, labelling them A, B and C. For each group, answer the questions that appear on the following list, marking the teams at some point on each scale.

As you read through this chapter, keep referring to your scores. The differences between these three teams that you know so well will give you a clearer insight into many of the issues we'll be discussing.

TEAM _____   TOTAL SCORE _____

1	The team is effective at getting things done	5	4	3	2	1	The team is ineffective at getting things done
2	Membership is vague and easy to achieve	5	4	3	2	1	Membership is defined and difficult to achieve
3	The team has clear standards of behaviour	5	4	3	2	1	The team has little influence on behaviour of its members
4	Individuals have clearly defined roles	5	4	3	2	1	There are no clearly defined roles
5	There are close personal relations within the team	5	4	3	2	1	Relationships are mainly impersonal

6	People share a clear concept of purpose	5	4	3	2	1	People have little understanding of team purpose
7	People feel a strong commitment to the team	5	4	3	2	1	There is little personal commitment to the team

Now let's look at the key questions to find out why some teams thrive, some merely survive, while others founder.

What is teamwork and why is it so important?

Teamwork is about individuals working together to accomplish more than they could alone – and then sharing the rewards. However, it's not just a question of strength in numbers. Teams come together to accomplish *more* than would be possible by individuals working on their own. This is achieved by harnessing, pooling and exploiting the resources available to the team – individual strengths, skills and experience – and by compensating for areas of individual weakness. One person's weakness is often another's strength, one person's ignorance another's expertise.

Working life is just too complicated to be negotiated comfortably by any one person acting in splendid isolation. And a good team is a great place to be: exciting, stimulating, supportive, successful – and fun! In an effective team, members take genuine pleasure in each other's successes, support colleagues' decisions, and willingly take their share of the blame when things don't work out – all vital ingredients in the motivational cocktail.

And, of course, not everyone is lucky enough to be in their job because they want to be there and nowhere else. The choice of job and workplace is more often dictated by circumstance – lack of appropriate qualifications to do another job; limited opportunities available in a particular region; the need to earn a 'living' wage etc. All this can make the task of building an effective and successful team quite challenging. However, it's worth the effort. Being part of a genuine team encourages people to believe they have a value beyond the routine of their day-to-day job, to feel that they belong and have an important part to play.

What's the difference between a group and a team?

A group can look very similar to a team – people working together, probably in the same place, maybe even with the same goal. But the crucial difference lies in the *way* they work together. In a team, all efforts are directed at a common aim, with every member co-operating to share expertise and maximise output. In a group, there's no mutual trust or defined goal that everyone shares. It is worth highlighting the important differences between how people work in groups and teams.

GROUPS	TEAMS
Individuals work independently	Time is not wasted struggling over territory
Members act like hired hands	Members feel ownership for their unit
Suggestions are not encouraged	Members apply unique talents to team objectives
Members distrust colleagues because they do not appreciate their role	Members can express ideas and opinions
Disagreement is seen as divisive	Disagreement is acceptable
Members are cautious about what they say	Members try to understand one another's point of view
Members don't know how to resolve conflict	Conflict is seen as an opportunity for new ideas and creativity
Members believe it's more important to do as others do than to produce positive results	Members participate in decisions aimed at achieving a positive result

What are the key indicators of a successful team?

How do you know that a team is working? This question can only really be answered by the team itself – two different teams may have very different ideas about what constitutes success. The best way to take the pulse of a team is to measure what it does, and see whether the members believe it's doing these things to the best of its ability. Have a look at the following list, and decide for yourself how your three teams (A, B and C) measure up.

- *Objectives and goals* Working in teams should be fun, but teamwork is much more than camaraderie for its own sake. You must be clear about what you want to achieve, and how you propose to accomplish the task. But what's the point of having objectives and goals if they are not clear to all members? The whole group has to know what it's aiming for, if people are going to show commitment and believe that this is a team worth belonging to. There's no possibility of achieving your goals or reaching your objectives, unless people accept that they are worth striving for. In an effective team, people give of their best and take what they need for the team. Are the objectives of your team well understood and accepted by all members?

- *Support and trust* Trust takes a long time to achieve, but can be destroyed in seconds. People will only trust others when they have confidence in their methods. You can expect three problems in this area:
  — people have different experiences, values and expectations which can colour their attitudes towards others;
  — competition for territory (turfism) makes people possessive and defensive;
  — people will become unhappy if you impose goals and performance standards on them, rather than seeking their involvement in advance.

  Trust and support will develop with time, provided people can talk freely about their fears, problems and their own limitations, and as long as they receive help and support from

70

others. Do your team members give each other a fair hearing? Can they rely on each other for support when the going gets rough?

- *Openness and confrontation*   With any group of people expressing opinions and ideas openly there's bound to be some conflict. And if you try to stop them stating their views in order to suppress differences of opinion, you'll take away their incentive to get really involved with the team's work. The secret is to balance these two interests. Your people need to feel confident that they can express themselves openly, without fear of ridicule or retaliation. But they also have to recognise that confrontation is expensive in energy and effort – both of which are needed for the team's creative work. How much discussion is there in your team? Does your presence inhibit discussion? Or are there other powerful players who stop conversation when they walk into a room?

- *Conflict and co-operation*   I've never come across a team totally untouched by internal politics and occasional flashes of bitchiness. They're part and parcel of office life and the wise manager accepts this. But you can – and should – aim to make sure that they don't take over. It's your job to intervene when things threaten to get out of hand. A gentle reminder that there's work to be done, and that you're not prepared to allow the team's work to be undermined by personality clashes or game playing, is generally sufficient. Conflict in itself, however, is not necessarily a problem and has a vital part to play in warding off complacency. Devil's advocacy can open up closed minds to new ideas, but people who dig their heels in and erect obstacles have just the opposite effect. If your people lose respect for each other, conflict and mistrust will begin to undermine the team's morale. So it's a question of balance. Do your people disagree openly? Is it common, but also relatively comfortable, to hear frank criticism being expressed? And what about personal attacks – are they tolerated? There's more about the management of conflict in Chapter 5.

● *Procedures and practices*   Efficiency and results are two important barometers of good teamwork. You want to make effective decisions, avoid duplication of effort and make the maximum use of your resources. So it's vital that everyone understands their role and their relationships with other members of the team. Are some members of your team being asked to do tasks that could be done more effectively by others? Is there overlap between different groups? Have you had a formal review of roles? If not, why not? These are questions any good team should be asking of itself – and of its leader.

● *Reviews*   You have to stand back and take stock of your team regularly. Can you still achieve the goals? What successes have you had? Any failures? Have the goalposts moved? On the basis of what's happened since your last stocktaking, what needs to be changed to make the team's performance more effective? Regular reviews don't just provide a vehicle for learning from experience, they should also rekindle people's interest in what's going on, provide an opportunity for redefining roles, resetting objectives, or doing whatever else seems to be necessary. Make reviews upbeat, enjoyable events. Turn them into social occasions, a reward for team effort, rather than just another meeting.

● *Individual development*   Although effective teamwork involves pooling skills, you'll want to recognise and develop the skills of individuals to give them the chance to make the most of their talents. It can only benefit the team to maximise each member's potential. Good managers encourage their people to appreciate each other's skills, and to share knowledge and experience unselfishly. Some of the most effective learning within organisations comes about as a result of effective teamwork.

● *Relations with other teams*   Your team will inevitably have to deal with other groups in the organisation. And just as your people need to work effectively together, so too must different parts of the organisation act together in the corporate interest – which occasionally means sacrificing team objectives. Where other teams rely on you for service, they should be treated with as much respect as you give customers outside the organisation. Be honest – how does your team match up to this demanding standard?

What are the symptoms of poor teamwork?

Everyone has some experience of being in a team that's not working properly. An outsider quickly gets the feeling there's something wrong with the atmosphere. People look frustrated and sound grumpy, not only with their colleagues, but with the very suggestion that they should all pull together. They've stopped being honest with each other and they refuse to admit mistakes. The chances are that they are also on a losing streak! In order to diagnose the state of health in a team I often use the following checklist. There are eight key variables and I give the team a rating of between 1 to 5 on each of them. You can use it to assess your team(s).

TEAM CHECK

LOSERS							WINNERS
Frustration, grumbling	Atmosphere	1	2	3	4	5	Honest, open, mistakes admitted
Backbiting, retaliation	Team relations	1	2	3	4	5	Healthy competition, support and trust
Open warfare	Relations with other teams	1	2	3	4	5	Constructive conflict, respect
Autocratically run, limited participation	Meetings	1	2	3	4	5	Democratic, creative, effective
Manager isolated, staff intimidated	Manager/staff relations	1	2	3	4	5	Contacts frequent, frank, fruitful
Static, moribund	Team members	1	2	3	4	5	Developing, optimistic

LOSERS						WINNERS
Unclear, unpublicised	Team's objectives					Widely understood,
	1	*2*	*3*	*4*	*5*	regularly reviewed
Rejected (the 'not	Attitude to outside help					Good ideas
invented here'	*1*	*2*	*3*	*4*	*5*	welcomed and
syndrome)						taken up

A team in perfect condition would score 40 points. Such teams don't exist! Thirty plus suggests that you're in pretty good shape, while a score of 20 or less indicates that there's work to be done. Have a look at the individual scores to find out where to start.

Research into how teams operate has pinpointed two special hazards to watch out for. Both of these can seriously jeopardise your team's effectiveness.

'Risky shift'

Contrary to the popular idea that committees are stuffy and conservative, a small group of people in a team will actually back riskier decisions than they would as individuals – particularly when the stakes are high. The reason for this is that being in a team encourages people to be bolder, not just because they are surrounded by supportive colleagues, but because they no longer feel personally responsible for the consequences of their decisions. If it doesn't work out, it'll be someone else's fault. The only problem is that everyone is thinking the same way. Hence the shift to risk.

So how can you avoid Risky Shift? Before any important meeting, get everyone to write down what they think the outcome of the discussion ought to be. Do not reveal or discuss these initial positions until the session is finished. Then check that the initial preferences have not been overruled by the group acting as a whole. If they have, backtrack to discover why and how.

The collective decision may, of course, be the right one. But it is vital to confirm that each member of the group is happy to bear responsibility as an individual for the final decision. They don't have to agree with it, but they must understand it and be committed to it.

'Groupthink'

Groupthink is another type of mass delusion which undermines the efficiency of small groups. It happens when people see the deficiencies in a plan, but don't point them out for fear of disrupting the group's harmony, hurting colleagues' feelings or being ostracised as trouble-makers or nit-pickers.

The smaller and more cohesive the group, the greater the danger of this taking place. It's particularly common in politics and whenever a group gets the feeling that the world is against it.

The easiest way to guard against Groupthink is to invite a neutral but respected outsider to evaluate the decision before reaching your final conclusion – whenever the importance of the issue justifies it.

How should you pick your team?

A team containing people with different views creates a useful diversity of opinion. It ought to improve the quality of decision-making and it will certainly increase your versatility. By contrast, cloning (i.e. selecting like-minded individuals who will fit in and can be relied on not to make waves) creates a cosy, but not particularly effective environment. If all your people have roughly the same world view, your team is not likely to grow or develop from its present position. A little criticism and disunity goes a long way towards keeping a team on its toes, and the right balance of personalities can make the difference between a winning and a losing team. Have a look at the following statements. Do any of them sound familiar?

- We're good on ideas but weak on implementation.

- We're not as co-ordinated as we could be. We may be strong on the control side of the job, but we don't adapt well to change.

- We need better back-up support for our field people. We just never look at the wider picture.

- We're very good at dealing with the task in hand, but lousy at communicating longer-term objectives.

- We need to involve more team members in decision-making.

All these statements suggest that there are positions unfilled in your team. The effective manager continually reviews the composition of the team, not just for individual strengths and weaknesses, but to check that all the vital functions are covered. Here's an exercise the team can do together to find out what people really think of each other.

1   Get each member of the team to answer the following questions. 'Who in this team would you choose . . .'
    to send on an important mission?
    to discuss a new idea with?
    as a sports companion?
    to ask for help if you were in serious trouble?
    to be marooned with on a tropical island?
    to escort your spouse/partner across the country?
    for a boss?

2   Then collate all their answers so that you have a complete list of who has been chosen for what and by whom.

3   Once you have got the results, here are some questions the team might like to consider together.
    Why were the choices made?
    Why do some names show up on the list more than others?
    Why are some people not chosen at all?
    Are opposites attracting or repelling each other?
    Does the exercise suggest any ways of improving the way you work together?

You can, of course, adapt this exercise by rewording the questions to reflect the current requirements of your team.

Having looked at the way people feel about each other, you should then return to the question of functions. What are teams actually supposed to do, i.e. what are their functions? You need to list them and make sure the team contains sufficient expertise to see that they're all carried out professionally. The psychologist Meredith Belbin has identified eight roles which he considers must be covered in every successful team. Review the make-up of your team in the light of these functions.

- *Resource investigator*   extroverted, enthusiastic, curious, communicative. Positive qualities include a capacity for contacting people and exploring anything new, with an ability to respond to challenge.

- *Completer-finisher*   painstaking, orderly, conscientious, anxious. Positive qualities are a capacity for following through and perfectionism.

- *Teamworker*   socially-oriented, rather mild, sensitive. Positive qualities are an ability to respond to people and situations, and to promote team spirit.

- *Monitor-evaluator*   sober, unemotional, prudent. Positive qualities include judgement, discretion and hard-headedness.

- *Plant*   individualistic, serious-minded, unorthodox. Positive qualities include genius, imagination, intellect and knowledge.

- *Shaper*   highly-strung, outgoing, dynamic. Positive qualities include drive and readiness to challenge inertia, ineffectiveness, complacency and self-deception.

- *Chairman*   calm, self-confident and controlled. Positive qualities include a capacity for treating and welcoming all potential contributors on their merits, without prejudice and with a strong sense of objectives.

- *Company worker*   conservative, dutiful, and predictable. Positive qualities are organising ability, practical common sense, hard work and self-discipline.

What categories do your people fall into? Do you have a broad enough range in the team or are you over-represented in some functions, dangerously light elsewhere? You should always evaluate your team in terms of its ability to carry out those activities that optimise performance. You don't have to have eight different people to carry out Belbin's eight functions. Some people will be able to represent several different functions quite adequately, but a well-rounded team does need to have cover in all the key areas. Here are some more questions to help you evaluate your people. Get everyone involved in answering and discussing them.

- How well does your team obtain the necessary information to do its work?

- How good is it at creating new ideas?

- How well does it explore new opportunities and promote itself and its ideas?

- How good is it at taking new ideas on board and developing them into working practice?

- How consistently does it achieve its goals and push for action?

- How good is it at ensuring that output is delivered on time, to accepted standards of effectiveness and efficiency?

- How well does it look after the detailed aspects of its work?

- How well does it maintain its standards, systems and procedures?

- Who co-ordinates your team's activities? Whoever it is (and it may well be you), are you satisfied that the job is being done adequately?

In the real world, it's not always possible to create a well-balanced team. Groups are often assembled on an *ad hoc* basis, and you're not given much choice about the selection of members. When you find yourself leading an outfit that resembles the Dirty Dozen, you have to live with it and try to compensate for any weaknesses, until such time as you can improve the situation.

Finally, let's see how all the members of your team, including you (the leader), shape up as team players. The following quiz is a test of their commitment to the ideal of teamworking, measured in the most direct way possible. People should be urged to be as honest as possible (I suggest anonymity for this exercise), because they are being invited to reveal the excuses they make for not behaving like a good team player.

I do not always involve my colleagues when I should because . . .

	TRUE	FALSE
I'm too busy	☐	☐
it takes too long to explain	☐	☐
it's more bother than it's worth	☐	☐
my problem is not their problem	☐	☐
they don't listen to me	☐	☐
when I need help they let me down	☐	☐
they criticise me	☐	☐
I have my job, they have theirs	☐	☐
they don't want my help	☐	☐
I don't know what they want	☐	☐

No one with more than two ticks in the 'True' column can call themselves a really committed team player. The team must decide whether it wants to break the pledge of anonymity or whether to keep discussion general. But most teams who carry out this exercise find plenty to talk about. It often emerges that someone who's been causing you real difficulty within the team is just not a team player. Perhaps they're an introvert or maybe they have a problem fitting in. You've created the perfect opportunity for discussing it with them, and for discussing a possible weakness in your team. And remember, even individualists can make a significant contribution to achieving the team's objectives – if they are used in the right way, in the right position.

How important is the leader?

Fish rots from the head down. That's not to imply that the only reason for a team's existence is its leader, but that quality of leadership affects the whole body of a team. Leaders are the medium through which goals are expressed, hopes and expectations channelled, and conflicts defused. It takes an enormous amount of physical and emotional energy to be a really effective leader. You have to get to know everyone in the team – how much do they value themselves, and how can you deploy them to best advantage? It will involve delegation and keeping an eagle eye on the team's objectives. Aim to cultivate the 'helicopter vision' that gives you a genuine overview of the situation.

The leader must recognise and exploit strengths, and compensate for individual weaknesses. Managing a team is a very different ball game from managing one to one, but managers must be good at motivating individuals before they can expect to get maximum value from the team. The aim is to create an environment of shared responsibility for getting results. A good team leader is a rare beast, not least because many of the qualities required appear to be almost mutually exclusive: highly intelligent, but not too clever; forceful, but sensitive to other people's feelings; dynamic, yet patient; effective as a persuader, but a willing subscriber to other people's ideas; a fluent provider of information, yet a good listener. This illustrates perfectly the key point about teams. Though not everyone will have all the required skills all of the time, the composite skills of the team will be available to all of the members all of the time – but only under effective leadership.

If your team is well balanced, with a variety of strengths and different personalities, does it really need a leader? The simple answer is – Yes! The fact is that a well-balanced team is not enough on its own. Diversity breeds conflict, and conflict requires guidance in order to achieve results and ensure high performance. Your role as a leader is to manage this aspect of teamwork. And because an effective team consists of players of very different abilities and personalities, the captain or leader needs to be able to bring out the best in everyone without introducing unnecessary aggravation based on accusations of favouritism or discrimination. Also, teams have to be picked, built and maintained in sound working order. The team leader must be strong enough to take in new blood and ensure that the team is able to cope with the departure of key players.

It is particularly important for you to demonstrate to your team that you know where you want them to go, how they are going to get there and what you expect each member of the team to achieve. This approach to leadership provides a firm base which allows you to:

- encourage participation, and agree objectives and targets;

- organise group-related tasks so members can co-operate and make their jobs easier;

- rotate jobs within groups so that members identify with the team as a whole, not just their own jobs;

- ensure that communications flow freely within and between groups;

- encourage informal meetings between groups to resolve problems.

Why bother with meetings?

Where teamwork is an alien concept, meetings tend to be run autocratically – when they happen at all. There may be an agenda, but it will be handed down from above and at the end of the session, there'll be several people who feel they've gained nothing from attending. An opportunity has been wasted, because meetings should of course be the lifeblood of your team. They are the perfect vehicle for encouraging creativity, motivating staff, boosting performance and allowing everyone to have a personal say in the pursuit of rewards. Meetings fall into several different categories and can have a variety of purposes.

Formal meetings

These can have two different functions: to share information and exchange views; or to set objectives and assign responsibilities so that decisions made elsewhere can be implemented.

Informal meetings

To keep the manager in touch with what's happening, but without interfering. This is a skill worth learning and practising. The great advantage of regular informal contact with people is that they learn how to communicate the key points of importance, so you are kept up to date with the project. How often do you meet informally with your team and how far down the line do you go?

Team briefings

A semi-formal meeting – a kind of management information system – which has become increasingly popular over the last few years. The objective is to ensure, on a regular basis, that all employees know and understand what is happening in the company and why.

The advantage of the team briefing system is that it enables face-to-face communications to be planned and conducted systematically, although the actual briefing sessions are conducted informally. People can then discuss with their line manager any company matters which affect them personally. Reasons for change are then brought into the open so that managers and staff are better informed, and better able to co-operate with any new developments.

Monitoring output

All teams have to produce results. However, if individual members are not aware of the group's overall direction, they may not work towards the same goals or give their best effort. Consequently, it is important to sit down with your team and discuss where you are heading. This means a team can focus its output and look for ways around obstructions.

Challenging targets

Teams need to have targets which are sufficiently structured to make the work interesting, but not so difficult that they cause despair. The successful manager will know how to achieve a balance by discussing the state of progress with the team. Are you shooting at the right targets? What do you need to do to keep ahead? You should encourage people to consider the new challenges they can set to improve not only their performance, but also that of the entire business.

Charting results

Identify the critical success factors, agree these with your team, then think of how best to measure them. It will act as a morale booster and a stimulus to further action if the whole team has a visible reminder of

where you are in relation to your goal. Teamwork is or
the end of improving performance, which can be meas...
results such as increased sales, reduced costs, improved proa...
better safety records, higher quality products or more new products.
There needs to be hard evidence of effective teamwork.

When team members seem to be dragging their feet in coming to
meetings, they obviously feel their time is being wasted. This could be
for any number of reasons. It is important to note that even if only one
member is not fully contributing to the effort, the effectiveness of the
team goes down dramatically, along with its potential for success. It
should be in every team leader's brief to find out why any individual
member is dissatisfied with the process of the meeting – and act on it!

Think back to your last two or three meetings and review how
they worked, and what they achieved. Ask yourself: as team leader,
were you guilty of putting up any of the following obstacles?

Did you:
> fail to listen to points made by others?
> constantly reiterate your own point of view?
> raise irrelevant and unhelpful points?
> concentrate on the impression you were making rather than on
> completing the task?
> constantly restate arguments instead of recognising them as
> alternatives?
> fail to participate?
> fail to be aware of the reaction of other members to your own
> contributions?
> fail to check how people were feeling about the discussion?
> fail to notice time spent?
> fail to be clear about what had been decided?
> try to go back and reopen a question which had already been
> decided?

As an aid to gaining commitment to a meeting, it's vital for people to
have an opportunity to talk about what they regard as important.
Make sure you ask your staff to put forward agenda items some days
before the meeting. Also, before the meeting starts, always ask
members if they wish to raise any additional matters. At least

two-thirds of the topics should involve everyone invited to the meeting. Look at the agendas of your last few meetings and consider the usefulness of the items discussed. You could also think about who decides how those items get on to the agenda. What's the best way to set an agenda which affects everyone at the meeting?

How can you tell whether your team is motivated?

Do you know how motivated your team is at the moment? Try this exercise to get a feel for the general atmosphere. Relying on your personal, subjective feelings, award marks on this checklist between the extremes of Very Poor and Excellent. Once you have marked your team yourself, try getting individual members of your team to do the same. The discrepancy between the scores may surprise you!

INDICATOR	Very poor				Excellent
How good is your team at achieving its targets?	1	2	3	4	5
How do you rate the team on dealing with failure?	1	2	3	4	5
What's the team like at handling conflict?	1	2	3	4	5
The meetings we have are . . .	1	2	3	4	5
The level of absenteeism from team meetings is . . .	1	2	3	4	5
The level of membership turnover in the team is . . .	1	2	3	4	5
How good are team members in passing messages?	1	2	3	4	5
How effective is the team in fostering suggestions?	1	2	3	4	5
How successful are our extracurricular events?	1	2	3	4	5
The way we handle team members' birthdays is . . .	1	2	3	4	5
The way we handle members leaving the team is . . .	1	2	3	4	5
The way we handle members joining the team is . . .	1	2	3	4	5

Though managing a team effectively can be very rewarding, it's never easy. Different people respond to different styles of management, and what's good for one person doesn't necessarily work for another. If you pride yourself on treating all your staff in exactly the same way, I'm afraid you're almost certainly preventing them from achieving their full potential. As we saw in Chapter 2, different folks *do* require different strokes.

Having said that, your policy on people's birthdays, for example, must be seen as fair and consistent. The challenge you face as a manager is to cater for individual preferences without incurring accusations of favouritism or discrimination.

In the management of the team, then, the team leader's greatest dilemma is in juggling three different principles: recognising individual differences, treating everyone fairly, while still motivating members individually. Motivation is the key to all three. Your team's drive and incentive will come from fair treatment, and the freedom to exercise their unique abilities, in a useful and productive way.

You'll know that you are succeeding when your team members stop moaning about the fact that you have scheduled yet another meeting – but make life very uncomfortable for you when you attempt to postpone the next project review!

Chapter 4

The Clever Stuff

Well-managed and motivated staff need to have their mental skills directed. A manager wants to harness all the intellectual resources available in the team, with a view to solving problems quickly, making sound and timely decisions, and encouraging innovation. He or she must also know how to exploit individual differences in learning styles if the team's full creative potential is to be realised.

The process of management can be seen as a never-ending exercise in problem-solving. The word 'problem' itself poses a problem. Its connotations are all negative – difficulty, anxiety, blame, trouble. But they don't need to be. People say they've got a problem when they can't see how to get from where they are to where they'd like to be. If the journey looks reasonably straightforward, they don't use the language of 'problems'. Instead, they talk about challenges and opportunities, management by objectives or other equally upbeat concepts.

The successful problem-solver has two main attributes: the appropriate knowledge or technical skill and the right mental attitude. Of course you must have the know-how to find the right solution, or at least have immediate, easy access to a source of such knowledge. But how you approach the problem is every bit as important. What is your first reaction when confronted by a problem? Here are three very common responses:

- 'Oh God, not again!'

- 'Why is this always happening to *me*?'

- '****! Still, I suppose that's what I'm here for.'

The first two responses are understandable, but are an unpromising start to solving problems. So far as the first is concerned, if there were no problems, it is very likely that there would be no need for managers. As for the second, it's unobservant at best, but at worst it's wildly off-beam. The person in the next office has just as many problems as you have. Only an idiot expects a problem-free working life. You have to accept this and stop taking problems personally. Instead, you need to see problems as a challenge to your professional competence, an opportunity to prove your worth. They are quite literally what your job is all about.

A problem should lead to positive thinking about what is to be done now, rather than to recriminations. Most problem-solving approaches involve four stages.

1   What exactly is the problem?
2   What possible solutions are there?
3   Which is the best possible solution?
4   What lessons have we learnt?

In this chapter, we shall discover what types of thinking are most likely to improve your chances of success at each stage of the problem-solving process. There are eight key questions.

1   How should you define – and respond to – problems?
2   What does creativity mean to you?
3   What are the barriers to creative thinking?
4   How can you develop your ability to think creatively?
5   How can you make the most of your team's thinking power?
6   Where does logic come in?
7   Why do we get decisions wrong?
8   Do you make problems pay for themselves?

Question 1 will help with Stage 1 of the problem-solving process. Questions 2 to 5 all bear on Stage 2. Questions 6 and 7 should help with Stage 3, while Question 8 is concerned with Stage 4.

How should you define – and respond to – problems?

In Stage 1 of problem-solving, you ask yourself, 'What is the problem?'. The problem has to be defined and key ingredients identified. Defining the problem is usually the hardest stage in the process. Remember the old cliché, 'Once you know what the problem is, you're half-way to solving it.'

There are various stumbling blocks at this stage: for example, defining the problem too narrowly or too broadly; or in terms which highlight inappropriate parts of it. If you haven't come across it before, try this 'nine dot' exercise, which illustrates the drawbacks of defining a problem too narrowly. Take a pen and join up the nine dots, without removing the pen from the paper, using four straight lines. You can intersect a line, but cannot retrace one.

The pitfall in trying to solve this problem is thinking within the square. (The problem can only be solved by extending a line outside the square. See page 159 for solution.) One technique for avoiding square-bound thinking in real life is to get several people to state how they see the problem area.

There is also a danger of thinking that you have cracked the problem of definition, and sticking too closely to your first effort. Things change, so it's essential to restate the whole problem frequently, in the light of what has been discovered. This process needs to be repeated until you have found a solution that matches the problem's current definition.

What does creativity mean to you?

Stage 2 involves generating ideas and solutions. First, by using old thinking – 9 times out of 10 this is all you have to do – then, if necessary, by using new thinking. This may involve using old channels in a new way and/or creating new channels, either deliberately or by happy accident.

What do you think about creativity? To find out, say whether you agree or disagree with the following 8 statements:

		AGREE	DISAGREE
1	*I am sometimes a creative person*	☐	☐
2	*Almost everyone is capable of being creative*	☐	☐
3	*Only exceptional people are capable of creativity*	☐	☐
4	*A good salesperson needs to be creative*	☐	☐
5	*A good scientist needs to be creative*	☐	☐
6	*The last time I persuaded someone to change their mind I was being creative*	☐	☐
7	*Creativity is the opposite of habit*	☐	☐
8	*Creativity helps you reach the 'right' answer*	☐	☐

Agreement with statements 1, 2, 4, 5, 6 and 7, and disagreement with 3 and 8, would indicate that you have an entirely positive attitude towards creativity, and subscribe to the view that it is 1 per cent about inspiration and 99 per cent about perspiration!

Some people are cynical about creativity. This is because the term has two different uses. Creativity can be thought of as an exceptional gift, for example when applied to the inspirational qualities of the likes of Picasso or Einstein. Alternatively, it can be seen as a characteristic all human beings possess, albeit in different quantities. In this sense, it refers to the capacity to change perceptions productively. When used like this, creativity is the opposite of habitual thinking.

People also get confused about the difference between creativity and innovation. Creativity is the thinking process that helps generate ideas, while innovation is the practical application of such ideas towards meeting the organisation's objectives in a more effective way (e.g. better, cheaper or more aesthetically). Creativity alone is never enough, since an idea is no more than the raw material for innovation. You need a systematic screening and development mechanism which converts ideas into tangible and valuable innovations. As a manager, you must create a climate in which there is both the scope to develop new ideas and the resources to implement them.

If you want to increase your team's capacity for creative thinking, there are three things to do.

● Understand the *barriers* to creative thinking.

● Develop your *individual capacity* for creative thinking.

● Use the *collective capacities* of others to develop new ideas by brainstorming.

What are the barriers to creative thinking?

The main barriers to creative thinking are:

● allowing your mind to be conditioned into following a *dominant pattern*, thus becoming trapped in a fixed way of looking at things – what Edward de Bono calls a 'concept prison';

● restricting the free growth of your ideas within *rigidly drawn boundaries*, which are treated as limiting conditions;

● failing to identify and examine the *assumptions* you make, to ensure that they are not restricting the development of new ideas;

● *polarising alternatives* – reducing every decision to an either/or when there may be other ways of looking at things;

● being conditioned to think *sequentially* rather than laterally and looking for the best idea, rather than different ideas;

● not *challenging* the obvious – the easy solution is so attractive;

● *premature evaluation*, i.e. not giving your imagination enough time to range freely over other ways of looking at things;

● a tendency to *conform*, and give the answer expected;

● the fear of *looking foolish* or being put down.

Mindsets

Most thinking on creativity and most problem-solving techniques stress the need for original and 'unrutted' thinking. The concept of 'mindsets' really refers generally to all the barriers that our minds erect to creative thinking. Mindsets blinker your perception, leading you to become stereotyped in the way you approach problems.

One powerful source of mindset is the presumption that your particular way of seeing yourself/your job/your organisation/your problems is the right and only way, that the world is as it is, and that no amount of thinking is ever going to change it. All the creative thinking techniques in the world won't shift somebody stuck in this kind of mindset. They'll be pessimistic about the possibility of change and resist all new ideas. Mindsets are self-fulfilling prophecies, since nobody ever managed to change themselves without believing that change is possible.

One reason why people fail to make the most of themselves involves their self-concept; that is the type of person you believe you are and the potential you believe you have. We touched on this mindset in Chapter 1 when discussing the irrational assumptions people hold. The problem lies in the phrase 'the potential you believe you have'. People can only achieve the potential that they *think* they have. It's clearly not true that anyone can do anything, but when you examine the reasons why they do less than they could, you usually find that the shortfall has more to do with their thinking than with their genetic potential. The mechanisms by which people only achieve what they believe to be possible is another example of a self-fulfilling prophecy. Studies show clearly that people work to the level expected of them, as well as to what they believe is their ceiling. So your view of yourself and other people's opinions can both be powerful obstacles to making the most of yourself.

Nowhere is this more true than in the matter of creativity. Many people have a fixed perception of themselves as non-creative, and are resistant to the notion of opening their minds when confronted by a problem. The real key to creativity is stating the obvious without being afraid of appearing boring. Don't be afraid to say something that someone else has said, because it may have acquired new significance. Something that seems very obvious to you may not be obvious to anyone else. Self-doubt leads to premature evaluation. Resist it, and work the way that suits you best. For example, if you don't feel confident with your creative ability, the worst situation for you to be in is a group brainstorm (see page 98). Don't refuse to take part, but do take 10 minutes to brainstorm on your own, then come back and make your contribution.

The influence of mindsets is not all negative. Mindsets can be used in a positive way in explaining the success of objectives. Many people have only a vague idea of their ideal life. Looking back, they notice opportunities they could have exploited. We are very good at 'if onlys'! If you take time to specify long-term aspirations, your mind will become alert to opportunities that can be exploited today, as opposed to the opportunities that were missed yesterday. The more specific the objective, the faster you'll notice the opportunity. So although mindsets are usually thought to blinker perception, they can also help to focus and sharpen it up, particularly when you're dealing with information. If you know what you are looking for, it's more likely that the relevant information will leap out from the pages of reports, memos etc. Mindset can be a useful protection against print fatigue.

How can you develop your ability to think creatively?

If you want to think more creatively, the first move is – inevitably! – a little self-analysis. Go through the list of barriers to creativity and ask, 'Is this me?' If it is, then think about the ways in which you can overcome the difficulty, concentrating on:

- breaking away from any restrictions;

- opening up your mind to generate new ideas;

- delaying judgement until you have explored the alternative ideas thoroughly.

In order to break away, you should:

- identify the dominant ideas influencing your thinking;

- define the boundaries you are operating within (e.g. experience, policies, procedures), and question them (Is past experience a reliable guide? Do the policies need rethinking? Do I still need to follow the procedure?).

In order to generate new ideas, you should:

● exploit the freedom you have won in breaking away by looking at the situation from as many different angles as possible;

● list alternative approaches without seeking the best one yet;

● trigger off new ideas by
   — *free thinking* – allowing your mind to wander over alternative, often apparently irrelevant, ways of looking at the situation
   — exposing yourself to *new influences* – people, articles, books, indeed anything that might bring new insight
   — *switching yourself* between problems
   — arranging for *cross-fertilisation of ideas* with other people
   — using *analogies* to spark off ideas.

In order to delay judgement, you should accept that evaluation is the enemy of generation. It's all too easy to kill off new ideas prematurely and to come up with plausible reasons for rejecting them.

For example:

● 'It couldn't work'

● 'It didn't work last time'

● 'It won't solve the problem'

● 'It's too risky'

● 'It's too expensive'

● 'It may be all right in theory, but . . .'

● 'The customers/boss/unions/shareholders will never buy it'

● 'It will create more problems than it solves'

● 'It wasn't invented here'.

You must also accept that objections – even valid ones – have no place until you have called a halt to the idea generation phase. In creative thinking it's the end result that counts and you shouldn't worry too much about the route you take to get there. It goes against the grain to delay judgement. But doing so is an important part of the discipline of creative thinking.

Techniques for fostering creative thinking

Incubation

The first technique is to rely upon the more intuitive and imaginative type of thinking, which psychologists tell us takes place in the right hemisphere of the brain. New insights in problem-solving often occur when analytical thinking has been put on the back-burner. Many of us have our best ideas when relaxing, walking, drinking, lying in the bath and so on. People who do crosswords describe waking up at 3 o'clock in the morning with the answer to 10 Across. The answers to every kind of problem, from simple riddles to highly complex technical matters, often occur when the mind is not directed at the problem.

Much problem-solving, writing and planning involves the *left* hemisphere. However, when the left side is at a lower ebb and the mind is more involved in spontaneous activities, or more relaxed, the right side seems to carry on working on the problem, which was originally presented by the left side. The right side then communicates useful insights to the left, where they are articulated and acted upon.

This explains why it is important to take time off or switch your attention to a completely different task when working on analytical problems or a piece of creative writing. Look at the quality of your writing occasionally, when you are under pressure. Give it – and yourself – a break, and see the improvement.

So the advice is, 'When in a state, incubate!'. Put the issue out of your mind for a while, if only overnight. Incubation helps in two ways: it gets the mind working unconsciously on the problem, focusing thoughts along the right lines, and when you return to the problem you'll be inspired by seeing it from a fresh angle, which may well bring you close to the solution.

Image-based techniques

Many managers find learning more difficult than they need to. When they're asked what sort of information they find easiest to remember, they point to: information which is humorous; information which they experience directly; information which is based on case studies; information where analogies and examples are given. These are all good examples of greater right hemispherical activity.

Image-based information can live on for years in the memory, only surfacing when the particular situation suddenly makes it relevant. The increasing use of experience-based training, case studies and video follows from realising that audiences need a combination of left (that is, verbal) and right (that is, more creative and directly experienced) information.

The human brain is an organ of almost unimaginable complexity and yet, when given a minute to think of all the uses a brick can be put to, many people come up with no more than six! Why? This task is a perfect illustration of how the left hemisphere can inhibit the right. Hearing the word 'uses', people restrict themselves to 'sensible' and 'existing' uses. But if every idea had to be both sensible and already in existence, where would new ideas, new products and original inventions come from?

In the 'uses of a brick' test, there is a simple way to generate unconventional, divergent thinking. Simply jot down as many objects as you can think of which bear no relationship whatsoever to a brick. For example, you might write down clock, cup, ashtray etc. How can you use a brick as a cup? Some bricks have the centre scooped out of them and you could use them as a birdbath or a drinking trough. How could you use a brick as a clock? As a sundial? How could you use a brick as an ashtray? In the same way as for a drinking trough? If you juxtapose any object with the brick, you can nearly always discover a particular use. Adopting this approach, within a minute you can probably jot down between 20 and 40 uses. If confronted by a specific problem, try getting new ideas by juxtaposing a totally unrelated idea. New channels emerge and then these are put back into the context of the problem. You simply replace the part of the problem with the unrelated object.

Lateral thinking

Edward de Bono's imaginative system aims to escape from habitual mind patterns ('vertical thinking'). Lateral thinking is not a single technique, but a system which includes various ways of assisting the creative leap to a new ('lateral') thought. These include the deliberate and provocative challenging of preconceptions and a rejection of yes/no thinking. Lateral thinking involves sideways leaps of imagination, rather than continuous progression down a logical chain of reasoning, and it encourages you to apply a different mindset to a problem, rather than following the usual ruts.

Logical (analytical thinking) is a step-by-step process. It is continuous; one step leading to the next, until you converge on the only possible solution. It is called vertical thinking, because you go straight down the line from one state of information to another. De Bono sums up the differences between vertical and lateral thinking, as follows:

VERTICAL THINKING	LATERAL THINKING
Chooses	Changes
Looks for what is right	Looks for what is different
One thing must follow direct from another	Makes deliberate jumps
Concentrates on relevance	Welcomes chance intrusions
Moves in the most likely direction	Explores the least likely

Creative thinking is not superior to logical thinking, just different. The best managers are both creative and logical. However strong they are on creativity, they must also be capable of applying logic in order to make good decisions.

The need to move between different modes of thinking is vividly illustrated by de Bono's six thinking hats. You have to separate emotion from logic, creativity from information and so on, and as you do so, you imagine putting on a different form of head-gear. Each represents one of the main types of thinking.

● *White hat thinking*   White hat thinking deals in facts and figures; it is neutral and objective. It has discipline and direction, but offers no interpretations or opinions. White symbolises its neutrality.

- *Red hat thinking*   Wearing the red hat allows the thinker to say how they *feel* about something. The red hat covers two broad types of feeling: ordinary emotions like fear, dislike and suspicion; and the more complex feelings involved in making judgements, such as hunch, intuition, taste and aesthetic feeling.

- *Yellow hat thinking*   Yellow hat thinking is positive and constructive, concerned with making things happen. It looks for value and benefits, and stands for sunshine, brightness, optimism and opportunity.

- *Green hat thinking*   Green hat thinking is creative. The colour symbolises fertility, growth and the value of seeds. The search for alternatives is the fundamental aspect of green thinking. The green hat thinking method generates new concepts and perceptions by getting out of our usual patterns of thinking.

- *Blue hat thinking*   The blue hat thinker organises the thinking process, defining problems and shaping questions. Blue hat thinking is responsible for summaries, overviews and conclusions, monitors progress and sees that the rules are followed.

- *Black hat thinking*   The black hat thinker points to what is wrong – to things that won't work, risks, dangers and design faults. The devil's advocate wears a black hat. Given our deep-rooted reluctance to look for evidence that contradicts our thinking, we cannot do without the black hat.

The thinking hats are a useful device to make sure that everyone is in the right mental mode at a particular moment. For example, at the beginning of a big project, you'll want the team to have their green hats on. Before you make a final decision, however, someone must have scrutinised the various options with their black hat firmly in place.

How can you make the most of your team's thinking power?

The hat technique is one way of getting your team members to adopt different roles. The important thing is for everyone to pick a role which suits their temperament. Working with someone who thinks in the same way as you do is easy and fun. But it tends to be less fertile than working with someone who thinks in a very different way from you. This can produce some discomfort, and it's important to give some thought to how the pain can best be handled and turned to advantage.

Problem-solving by a team does not guarantee better solutions than those reached by its members working in isolation. Complex tasks, however, are usually easier to solve when a pool of experience has been brought to bear by members of a team working together co-operatively. The price you pay for co-operation is conflict. A body of facts should be worked out in advance, to prevent conflict arising in the early stages of problem-solving. Differences of opinion are bound to arise – and are welcome – in the interpretation/evaluation phase, and it is the manager's job to act as referee and ensure that good-natured debate does not degenerate into a bloodbath.

Brainstorming is the most widely-used technique for making the most of a team's problem-solving potential. Its objective is to counteract the tendency to overlook potentially useful options while searching for new ideas. Mainly taught as a group technique, it can also be a good discipline for individuals. Its key principle is to defer judgement. This is achieved by writing down all ideas put forward before making any attempt to classify or evaluate them. Normally we formulate a problem and evaluate each idea likely to form a solution as it springs to mind. Brainstorming, however, employs the principle of 'quantity first, quality later'. It's an easy technique to learn and can be applied to almost any type of problem for which new ideas are needed.

The fundamental principles of brainstorming are:

- *quantity of ideas* – the amount is paramount, the target being as many as possible;

- *freewheeling* – uninhibited self-expression, seeing how things develop without hindrance;

- *suspension of criticism* – opposition, attacks and disapproval only restrict the pool of opinions;

- *deferment of judgement* – don't start to consider the merits and demerits until you're convinced there are no more ideas to be found.

Here are the main features of brainstorming.

- A small group (usually between 6 and 12 people) is assembled. If you have less than 6, you may lose out on skills/expertise relevant to the problem, and with more than 12, there's a risk of people feeling intimidated and not saying what they think.

- As far as possible, members should be selected to give the broadest range of skills and experience. But be tactful when composing the group, because people who are excluded may feel snubbed and subsequently try to undermine the fruits of the group's endeavours.

- A leader is elected to outline the rules and see that they are followed.

- It may be necessary to have a warm-up session to allow the group to become familiar with the procedure.

- The leader states the problem, being careful not to define it too narrowly.

- The leader opens the session by a phrase like, 'In how many ways can we . . .?', and then encourages people to contribute. The leader resists any attempt to evaluate ideas and restates the problem from time to time.

- A notetaker condenses the ideas suggested and writes them on a flip chart. The notetaker does not attempt to edit or eliminate duplications at this point.

- The leader continues to elicit contributions from the group, encouraging people to freewheel and come up with as many ideas as possible – good, bad, indifferent, sensible or silly. The leader keeps the pace up, and never comments or allows anyone else to comment on contributions. Every idea is accepted.

● The leader closes the meeting after 30 minutes or so, 45 at the outside.

● Evaluation takes place later, possibly with a different group. At this session, the aim is to select ideas for immediate use, identify ideas for further exploration, and review any different approaches which have been revealed by the session.

Brainstorming is a useful technique for releasing ideas, overcoming inhibitions, cross-fertilising ideas and getting away from patterned thinking. It needs to be planned and executed carefully, and there must always be proper evaluation of what has been achieved. It won't solve all your problems, but it can help you crash through barriers erected by traditional approaches to decision-making. To make it work for you, you really have to keep going during the first phase. There's a danger of finding an early suggestion too attractive, or of simply giving in to boredom or fatigue. In a brainstorming session we ran recently with the board of a large financial institution, the suggestion that finally provided the answer was number 63!

Remember that while techniques for increasing creativity help break new ground, you will also need to weigh up the pros and cons carefully before endorsing decisions. Remember, too, that there is another source of creativity within your team that you may not yet be fully exploiting – the sheer *variety* of thinking styles different members will be bringing to the party.

We are not really taught to think. Most of us stick to haphazardly acquired mental habits and know only what is familiar to us. We don't often try other methods and we are largely unaware of the different thinking styles that other people employ. As a result, if you walk into a colleague's office and see her gazing out of the window, you may assume that she is day-dreaming. If it were you, the fact that you were not actively doing anything would mean that you were not engaged in productive thought. Your colleague, on the other hand, may think most effectively when she doesn't appear to be on the ball. Similarly, one colleague may prefer to think on his feet and respond immediately to a question, while another may say, 'Give me half an hour and I'll get back to you'. The effective manager must observe and remember what produces the best results for each member of the team.

However you do your best thinking, it's imperative to build thinking time into your planning. Thinking has to be part of your repertoire. If you refer to the section on time management (page 52), you may well find that thinking time is something you don't allow for. It requires discipline to programme it in – for yourself and for other members of the team. But you'll need to do it to get the most out of them – and you.

Where does logic come in?

You will remember that Stage 3 of the problem-solving process involved identifying the best possible solution, by coolly analysing and deciding between all the alternatives. We saw earlier that the brain is divided into two halves, each having a specific function. By exploiting the different abilities of each section, and by understanding their separate powers, you can increase your thinking power. But we also agreed that creativity without analysis can result merely in day-dreams. In business, as in art or science, it is the interaction between the two thinking styles that produces the creative leap forward.

Clear or logical thinking is the process by which one judgement is derived from another and correct conclusions are drawn from the evidence. Clear thinking is analytical: it involves sifting information, selecting what is relevant, and establishing and proving logical rela-tionships. If you say something is logical, you simply mean that reasonable inferences are being drawn. Conclusions can be proved by the facts used to support them and a clear thinking, logical approach to problem-solving, decision-making and case presentation is an essential attribute of the effective manager.

Clear thinking involves three stages.

Developing a proposition

The facts must be relevant to the issues under consideration. If comparisons are being made, like must be compared with like. You have to dig deep, take nothing for granted and discard irrelevant

101

evidence. Where possible the connection between facts and conclusion should be justified on the basis of verifiable experience.

Testing propositions

When forming a proposition, you generalise from what is observed. If your proposition is derived from a generalisation based on particular instances, you must test it by answering the following questions.

- Was the scope of investigation sufficiently comprehensive?

- Are the instances representative or selected to support a point of view?

- Are there contradictory instances that have not been looked for?

- Does the proposition conflict with other beliefs, equally well supported?

- If there *are* conflicting beliefs or contradictory items of evidence, have they been put to the test against the original proposition?

- Could the evidence lead to other equally valid conclusions?

- Are there other facts that have not been taken into account which may have influenced the evidence and hence the conclusion?

Reasoning

The two most common types of reasoning are inductive and deductive. With inductive reasoning, the conclusion is highly probable, but not necessarily true. Connections are made by moving from the particular to the general, and the less general to the more general. Sherlock Holmes, for example, used inductive reasoning to solve his cases.

Induction can be a very dangerous process, especially when you make false connections as a result of prejudice or bias. Take the following example: 'My wife doesn't listen to me. She is a woman. My new manager is a woman. She probably won't listen to me.'

In deductive reasoning, the move is from the more general to the less general, and from the general to the particular. In a valid deductive argument, the truth of the premisses guarantees the truth of the conclusion. So deduction is only misleading if one of the original premisses is false: 'My wife has never listened to anyone in her life. People ought to listen to their partners. Therefore I must divorce my wife.'

In both deductive and inductive reasoning people experience great difficulty in using negative information, i.e. what is *not* the case. The problem here is that we are used only to experiencing what *is* the case. In *The Silver Blaze*, Sherlock Holmes asks Inspector Gregory to consider the curious incident of the dog in the night time. The mystified and slow-witted policeman replies, 'The dog did nothing in the night time', to which Holmes replies triumphantly, 'That was the curious incident'. Had the dog barked at the intruder, it would have proved little. Holmes's formidable intellect allowed him to see that the fact that the animal had remained mute strongly suggested that the intruder was someone the dog knew.

Logic is misleading when it involves a fallacy. Here are the most common fallacies.

- *Generalisations* are invalid when produced by over-simplifying the facts or selecting instances that favour your view while ignoring those that conflict with it. For example, 'All Italians are criminals – I know, because I was once ripped off in a shop in Florence.'

- *Potted thinking* involves the use of slogans and catch-phrases. For example, 'Well, you would say that, wouldn't you?'

- *Special pleading* happens when you lose objectivity and fail to consider alternatives. For example, 'Everyone knows that our department handles this sort of problem better than anyone else.'

- *Over-simplification* is a particular instance of potted thinking or special pleading. You insist that a sharp line be drawn, when in fact no sharp line can be drawn. For example, 'Everyone who is not for us is against us.'

- *Begging the question* involves taking for granted something that has yet to be proved. For example, 'You should use our product because the best product gives the best results.' It may do, but you haven't yet demonstrated that yours *is* the best.

- *False analogy*. Analogy forms the basis of much of our thinking. We notice that two cases resemble each other in certain respects and then assume that everything that applies to one must apply to the other. For example, 'If the Ritz reckons it needs a harpist playing at breakfast, we'd better get one here at Fawlty Towers.'

Why do we get decisions wrong?

How can you improve your ability to make decisons? Here are some suggestions, most of which flow from what has been discussed earlier.

- *Improve your analytical ability* A complicated situation can often be resolved by separating the whole into its component parts. Analysis should relate to facts, though when trying to understand the root causes of a problem, you may have to start with opinions. Even if you ask people to search for facts first, they will probably look for those which fit their preconceptions. However, opinions are an acceptable starting point, as long as they are tested against reality.

- *Adopt a systematic approach* Analyse the situation, identify possible courses of action, weigh them up and decide what to do. Don't seek a bland consensus. The best decisions often emerge from a clash of viewpoints.

- *Use your imagination* A strictly logical answer to the problem may not be the best one. Use lateral thinking, analogies and brainstorms to get out of the rut.

- *Keep it simple* One of the first principles of logic is known as Occam's Razor, which states that entities should not be multiplied unnecessarily. Or, to put it more simply, if you see four hoof-prints in the dust, start with the assumption that they were made by one horse, rather than two standing on their hind legs!

● *Implementation*   A problem has not been solved until a decision has been implemented. Think carefully not only about how a thing is to be done, but also about its impact on the people concerned and the extent to which they will co-operate. You will get less co-operation if you impose a solution. Ideally, everyone involved would arrive jointly at a solution all agree is best suited to the situation (more on this in Chapter 5).

Some managers thrive on decision-making. It was said of one celebrated 'decision junkie' that he loved making decisions so much he would make and remake the same decision 10 times in an afternoon! Most managers have mixed feelings about decisions. They are afraid of getting them wrong, and the more people likely to be affected by their actions, the more anxious they become. Often you have to decide in a hurry and don't have the time to analyse every conceivable solution. The temptation is to fix on the quickest, easiest or just the first answer that presents itself. Such short-cut methods are unlikely to produce the best results. Here are some other reasons why we don't always make good decisions.

● *Bias*   The natural inclination is to focus on/remember/notice those things that support your current beliefs. Prejudice can easily blind you to hidden drawbacks.

● *Habit*   Because you have always had a cigarette at the firm's Christmas dinner in the past, you don't have to assume that you always will.

● *Intuition*   Hunches based on subconscious instincts ('I feel it in my bones') rule out true investigation. They may provide a starting point, but they must not be allowed to preclude the pursuit of alternative options.

● *Wishful thinking*   It's always a mistake to confuse what is the case with what you'd like it to be. What you find desirable or convenient may well be the wrong answer, and the more you are attached to it, the less likely you are to question it or seriously explore the downside.

● *Euphoria*   Again, feeling too enthusiastic about a course of action can easily cloud your better judgement.

● *Saving face*   Time, money and resources are too often wasted trying to justify or stay with a bad decision. You need to be prepared to cut your losses, and to give yourself a chance to retrieve the situation after making a bad decision. We all get some decisions wrong. The lady may not be for turning, but a good manager is always prepared to consider that possibility.

● *Need for instant answers*   Ambiguity and indecision can cause stress, so it's easy to reach the conclusion that any decision is better than none. This is rarely the case.

● *Stress*   Common symptoms of stress include an impaired ability to listen, an over-focused vision (tunnel vision), forgetfulness, mental block and an inability to concentrate.

Do you make problems pay for themselves?

The final stage of the problem-solving process is concerned with learning lessons, drawing conclusions and generally taking all steps possible to ensure that the problem cannot recur. At the beginning of this chapter, I referred to the importance of attitude towards problems. Good managers regard them not merely as a challenge, but as a valuable source of material on how to improve the quality of their operation. This involves the technique of interrogating a problem. Once it has been solved to your satisfaction, instead of sweeping the issues under the carpet, you nail the problem down, shine a bright light on it and refuse to let it go until you have learnt everything it can tell you about why it happened and what you could have done to prevent it.

Most people assume that they learn from life. What they mean is that they acquire new knowledge, rather than new ways of doing things. Most of us tend to swing haphazardly between different approaches. When things are ticking over satisfactorily, we get complacent and just assume that we are learning as much as we need to. Then something happens to shatter the complacency and we talk about learning a painful lesson. Sometimes we're more selective and use hindsight to review a particular experience in order to learn a particular lesson. On other occasions, we deliberately try out different ways of doing things in order to learn.

Understanding how to learn from experience and accepting that different people have different preferred learning styles are two vitally important management skills. What is the most effective way to learn from experience? According to psychologist Dr Peter Honey, learning from experience involves four stages.

1 *Having the experience*   You can either let the experience come to you (reactive) or you can deliberately seek it out (proactive).

2 *Reviewing the experience*   This means looking back over what has happened without being judgemental. If you are caught in the activity trap, you are restricted to learning to cope, rather than learning from experience. You may become an expert fire-fighter, but you will never become a great strategist.

3 *Concluding from experience*   The object of reviewing experience is to draw sound conclusions. This needs to be distinguished from jumping to conclusions. It involves carefully scanning the raw material assembled in the reviewing stage. It helps if the conclusions are specific.

4 *Planning the next steps*   Planning involves translating at least some of the conclusions into a programme for appropriate future action.

The chances are that you are currently performing much better at some stages in the process than at others, as a result of your individual learning style. There are four such styles. To discover which of these you prefer, answer the following questions. You must answer 'Yes' or 'No' to each of them. When you are uncertain, just tick whichever answer is closer to your view.

		YES	NO
1	Do you thrive on surprises and the unknown?	☑	☐
2	Does it cause you pain to have to make decisions under the pressure of tight deadlines?	☑	☐
3	Do you get irritated by colleagues who refuse to take things seriously?	☑	☐
4	Do you get impatient with people who can't make up their minds quickly enough?	☐	☑
5	Do you live for the present?	☐	☑
6	In a meeting, do you prefer to listen to other people's opinions rather than talk yourself?	☑	☐
7	Do you believe that if a job's worth doing, it's worth getting absolutely right?	☑	☐
8	Do you always read all the instructions on a new piece of equipment?	☑	☐
9	Do you believe that 'who dares wins'?	☑	☐
10	Do you get irritated by people who are always rushing into things?	☐	☑
11	Do you always insist on thinking through a problem step by step?	☐	☑
12	In meetings, do you often find yourself getting annoyed by people who indulge in idle speculation?	☑	☐
13	Do you believe that the best ideas tend to come from gut feelings?	☐	☑
14	Do you always consider all the options before coming to a decision?	☑	☐
15	Generally speaking, do you get on best with logical, analytical people?	☐	☑
16	Do you believe that the ends generally justify the means?	☐	☐
17	Are you a better talker than a listener?	☐	☑
18	Do you pride yourself on your sense of objectivity?	☑	☐
19	Does it infuriate you when people change their plans on impulse?	☐	☑
20	Do you believe that the feelings of individuals must always take second place to achieving the team's objectives?	☑	☐

There are four different types of learner.

- *The Activist: 'I'll try anything once'*   Activists seek out and throw themselves enthusiastically into new experiences. They enjoy the here and now, are open-minded and free from scepticism. They are Action Men and Women. They tend to act first and consider the consequences later.

- *The Reflector: 'I'd like time to think about it'*   Reflectors like to stand back and observe what's going on from different perspectives. They are great analysts, but slow to draw conclusions. Caution is their byword and they prefer to keep a low profile.

- *The Theorist: 'How does this fit with that?'*   Theorists integrate their observations into sound theories. They think problems through in a vertical, step-by-step fashion. They are perfectionists who won't rest easy until things fit their rational schemes.

- *The Pragmatist: 'How can I apply this in practice?'* Pragmatists like to try out new ideas, theories and techniques to see if they work. They come back from management courses brimming with new schemes. They like to get on with things and aren't always patient with lengthy discussions.

Questions 1, 5, 9, 13 and 17 all tap the Activist learning style. Score two points for every 'Yes' you ticked for these questions. Follow the same procedure for questions 2, 6, 10, 14 and 18 for your Reflector score; questions 3, 7, 11, 15 and 19 for the Theorist style; and 4, 8, 12, 16 and 20 to assess your preference for the Pragmatist approach.

You will probably find that you have scored significantly higher on one or two learning styles than on the others. Since all styles are useful at different stages of the learning cycle, it's clearly worth while trying to modify your approach so as to boost your enthusiasm for the styles that don't come to you naturally. By embracing 'alien' ways of approaching problems, you'll be able to cope successfully with a wider range of situations. You will spend less time feeling like a fish out of water, and you'll have gained an insight into other people's learning methods. Reginald Perrin's boss C.J. would probably deny this ('I didn't get where I am today by embracing alien ways of approaching problems'). But he is wrong. You can certainly get by in specific circumstances with just one style of learning. But circumstances shift continually in the business world, and these shifts can only be comfortably handled by versatile and flexible managers.

In the same way that new solutions to problems may strike you as you change from 'red hat' to 'black hat' thinking, it can only help to swap learning styles. The Activist can learn from the Theorist that step-by-step analysis is sometimes the best approach, while the Pragmatist can teach the Reflector to let go and try something new.

To gain a clearer perspective on the way you learn, try keeping a record of significant problems and what you learned from them. Start by thinking back over the experience and writing a detailed description of what happened during that period. Then, list the conclusions you reached as a result. These conclusions are your learning points, and should form the basis of an action plan to avoid the same problems in the future. You may decide that you need to spend more time on planning, or less time on deliberating. Keep the points specific, as you will need to refer to them as we move on to the next vital stage – making things happen.

Before we do this, however, let's end this complex chapter on a lighter note. These days, all managers worship at the altar of the great god 'Innovation'. In a changing environment, of course we all have to learn to love change and apply as much creativity as we can muster to our businesses. People at the top of organisations, who have most to lose, lead the charge. They are always asking for bright ideas, starting suggestion schemes and generally inviting more participation. But do they really listen? Here is a cynic's version of 'The Boss's Guide to Innovation'.

- Treat any new idea that comes from below with suspicion. After all, it is new – and it comes from below.

- Insist that anyone who needs your approval before they can act has first to go through several lower layers of management. After all, a good story can only improve in the telling.

- Encourage departments and individuals to challenge and criticise each other's proposals. This saves you hours of tedious decision-making. You just pick the survivor.

- Don't hesitate to express your criticisms freely, but go easy on the praise. This keeps people on their toes. It also does no harm to remind them that they can be fired at any time.

- When a subordinate identifies a problem, leave them in no doubt that you regard it as a sign of failure. This will discourage people from letting you know when something in their area isn't working in future.

- Control everything with the utmost care. Make sure that people count anything that can be counted – frequently.

- Always make decisions about reorganisation or a change of policy in secret. Spring them on people unexpectedly. This too keeps people on their toes.

- Make sure that any request for information is fully justified. After all, you don't want data falling into the wrong hands – especially if those hands belong to one of your managers.

- Always make lower-level managers responsible for figuring out how to cut back, lay off, move people around or otherwise implement threatening decisions that you have made. Get them to do it quickly, and tell everyone that you are acting like this because you believe in delegation and participation.

- Above all, never forget that you, the boss, already know everything important about your business. Otherwise you wouldn't be the boss, would you?

Chapter 5

Making it Happen

There's nothing more frustrating than knowing exactly what needs to be done, but not being able to make it happen. You probably know the situation. The project was right up your street, your research was thorough and your recommendations were imaginative but eminently practical. You had exactly the right people to carry it through and the timing looked perfect. And what happened? Nothing.

Why do things not happen when they should? It really is the $64,000 Question for a manager, because you are judged by results. All that careful planning, the creative energy you unleashed and the wave of enthusiasm you generated count for nothing if you fail to deliver. So there's a piece missing from the 'How do you Manage?' jigsaw. To supply it, we need to start by examining why things that ought to happen don't. Here are some of the most common reasons:

- the situation changes or somebody moves the goalposts;

- promised resources are withdrawn;

- some cataclysmic, unpredictable event occurs;

- there are changes in key personnel;

- the wrong person is appointed to lead the project;

- no one is willing to lead the project;

- so much effort went into preparation, there's none left for implementation;

- it's so obviously right, nobody bothers to convince other people;

- the sheer size of the thing deters people from taking the first step;

- it has head-appeal, but leaves the heart cold;

- the sponsor has enemies (or a single influential opponent);

- inexplicably, a sufficient head of steam never builds up.

It's impossible to make contingency plans for literally everything that might happen. What you can do is remember – and act upon – what's happened in the past, keep yourself as well informed as you can about everything that's going on currently and then make intelligent guesses about what's likely to happen in the future. The effective manager's response to a list of obstacles is equally pragmatic. You waste no time on those that are totally beyond your control. Instead, home in on those you can do something about. In the list above, there's at least one Act of God, the sort of thing you just can't anticipate or remedy. But all the rest can – and should – be avoidable by careful planning, professional presentation and the application of certain key psychological skills. It also helps to have deep reservoirs of determination, persistence and courage.

Here are some important questions.

1 Do you understand the art of influence?
2 Are you an effective communicator?
3 Why do we get our wires crossed?
4 Do you know how to negotiate?
5 What do you do when things don't happen?

Do you understand the art of influence?

The art of influence is all about selling ideas, persuading people that your point of view is the right one and that what you want to happen is what *they* want to happen – and want to help you bring about. There are some techniques involved – selling, presentation, communication, negotiation and so on – but the key to success lies in your attitudes and aspirations. No one ever succeeded in convincing anyone of anything without first selling themselves on the idea.

Selling ideas is very much like selling anything else. As a result, people who are best at wielding influence tend to have pretty sophisticated selling skills. But what makes a good sales person? Research into the differences between successful and unsuccessful sales people reveals that people who are best at selling:

- spend more time planning and organising;

- are better judges of people;

- are more accomplished at forming close personal relationships;

- are higher on empathy;

- are more flexible and comfortable with a wider range of personality styles;

- control their moods better (i.e. no extravagant rejoicing at success or expressions of despair at failure);

- are less likely to take the rejection of their ideas as a personal affront.

Successful sales people are also willing to take calculated risks, are good at time management, follow things through, have the imagination to see their way round obstacles and realise that there's no general rule which says that the hard or the soft sell is more effective. They are particularly skilful, however, at appreciating which is the more appropriate on a particular occasion.

Recent research also pinpoints the characteristics of the *great* sales person. They are self-starting, action-oriented with a 'can do' philosophy, and they're ambitious – though not at the expense of their integrity. They also act and sound like winners – people who are confident they can make things happen. You can hear the difference between winners and losers in the way they respond differently to the same situation. Have a look at the abbreviated 'Dictionary of Winnerspeak and Losertalk' below. Do you sound like the sort of person who can make things happen?

WINNERSPEAK	LOSERTALK
Let's find out	Nobody knows
I'm good, but I could be better	I'm better than some people
That's a piece of luck	That's typical of my bad luck

WINNERSPEAK	LOSERTALK
Tell me what you think	Let me tell you what I think
I look at that person's success and I say good luck to them	That person is so successful, it makes me sick!

Where technique is concerned, people who are good at selling their ideas attribute their success to the following five principles.

- *Be prepared* This refers to your material, your audience and yourself. Whatever the material (from a massive report to a one-page memo), and however it is to be communicated, it has to be clearly and coherently assembled, and presented in such a way as to appeal to the particular audience. This will involve researching the audience in advance, to find out its current position on the issues being addressed, to anticipate likely objections and to pre-sell any controversial suggestions. As regards your own performance, you need to be sure that you are playing to your strengths and not exposing your weaknesses. An important presentation will probably involve other members of the team. Make sure that they too are making the contribution they are best equipped to offer. Be careful that everyone understands their role. Otherwise there's a danger of people assuming that someone else is taking responsibility for putting the central message across, and a risk of confusing the audience.

- *Be focused* Make sure you know exactly what you want to achieve and why. What's the most you can hope for, and the least you'd be prepared to accept as a successful resolution? If you're making a formal presentation, don't allow the meeting to be hijacked by someone with an axe to grind. As the person who wants things to happen, it's your job to see that the meeting follows its ordained course and reaches its inevitable outcome. Make it easy for them to give you what you want. Let them see that it's in their interest too. Expose the downside and show them how to cope with it. And when you have got agreement in principle, try and convert it into action immediately. You may not be able to get them to sign the cheque then and there, or leave with a complete timetable. But you must, at the very least, aim for minuted action points and a date for the first follow-up meeting.

● *Be flexible* This sounds like the opposite of being focused. It is! Like so many other aspects of the manager's job, you need a preferred strategy and a fall-back position. Occasionally, things go exactly as you planned – a triumph for your focused thinking. But it's more prudent to expect the unexpected and to have Plan B tucked away in your back pocket (ideally, along with Plans C to Z!).

● *Be convinced* Just as sales people rarely give of their best when they lack confidence in the product they represent, so you should always try and avoid having to put a case you don't believe in. The ideal situation is selling your own ideas in your own words. Quite often you'll find yourself having to sell other people's ideas, but you're never obliged to read their text – literally or metaphorically. In fact, it's always best to rework other people's ideas and material if you have to present them. If you are in the awkward position of having to sell a decision you were opposed to, it's imperative that you make your U-turn in private and arrive at the presentation ready to make the case with conviction.

● *Be convincing* Effective presentations sound balanced. You need to be able to give arguments against your position in order to refute them. Search for common ground with potential opponents and build on it. Exploit the law of office life which states that, other things being equal, most people will agree to a reasonable request (they know it won't be long before they're asking you for a favour). Be aware that if you come on too strong you run the risk of being turned down completely, and that if you sound as though you are acting out of vested interest, people will suspect your motives. Encourage the audience to participate. The more they do, the more convinced they'll be of your case – why else would they be bothering to contribute? Crude manipulative devices can work in the short term: for example, such classic selling

116

ploys as 'foot in the door' (a small request followed by a large one), 'door in the face' (large request followed by a small one) or 'low ball' (going back on your part of the bargain). But people resent being duped and made to feel foolish. You may have tricked them into agreement, but they will do their utmost to stop you implementing your plans.

In Chapter 1 we saw how we are limited by our expectations of ourselves. However, other people's expectations of us can be turned to advantage. Celebrated winners always start with an advantage over their opponents, and the way to get a reputation for being a mover and a shaker – the sort of person who makes things happen – is to accept and act upon the motto 'Who sells, wins!'. But never under-estimate the importance of timing. You need to catch your audience in the right mood or, if necessary, create the right atmosphere, before getting down to the business of selling. You must be in the right mood, too. Here's a simple exercise to check your frame of mind before going into battle. Your objective should be to give a decisive thumbs down to each of these statements.

- 'Good ideas sell themselves.'

- 'I only do things when success is guaranteed.'

- 'It's best to keep any really important information to yourself.'

- 'I spend a lot of time thinking about my failures.'

- 'I love it when other people fail.'

- 'I need other people to tell me when I've been successful.'

- 'Competent people are a real threat to me.'

Are you an effective communicator?

As a manager, you will know that communication is the most important weapon in your armoury. Sadly, you are probably also familiar with an unfortunate design flaw it possesses: no matter where it's aimed, it tends to direct bullets into the foot of the person pressing the trigger! Looking back over all the employee attitude surveys I've carried out, I can't think of a single management team that escaped a hammering for its deficiencies in the communication department – or one that didn't believe the attack was unjust!

Every manager knows the problem. There's no mystery about the solution, either. As with selling, there are technical skills involved – writing and presenting effectively, handling meetings, listening and so on – but successful communication starts from accepting a simple principle. This is that the communicator has total responsibility for getting the message across. This doesn't mean that I think audiences are passive, just that they don't have to listen to you or accept what you're saying. It feels unfair – an irritating, often frustrating situation, but it's one that effective managers know they must accept if they are to succeed. Communication lies at the heart of the management task, precisely because it's the key to making things happen.

That's why the safest attitude towards communication is probably one of baffled humility, captured in the classic observation, 'I know you believe you understand what you think I said, but I'm not sure you realise that what you heard is not what I meant'. Of course, both sides make mistakes, but it's the communicator who has the incentive and the responsibility to transmit the message. So let's focus on the technical skills mentioned above, all of which can help you communicate more effectively.

Written reports

A good report is easy to recognise because it leaves the reader with two positive feelings:

● there's something in this for me;

● that report was a piece of cake to read.

Here are five suggestions to help you reach this ideal outcome.

Get the story straight

Every report has a story to tell. Make sure you tell it clearly and vigorously. Before starting, make sure you know what you want to say. It shouldn't take more than a paragraph to write down all the main points. Refer to it frequently to make sure you're not deviating from your central message. To grab and keep the reader's attention, you'll need to know what they want from the report – an analysis of a problem, a source of information to refer to or a firm recommendation.

Put the last page first

Even when no recommendations are required, your report must have clear conclusions. Readers will turn to them first and may read no further if the conclusions don't capture their interest. The main analysis comes next, with details held back for the appendices. This isn't the logical way to write, but it's what the reader wants. A side benefit of putting the last page first is that it encourages you to keep the report brief.

When in doubt, leave it out

Short reports are easier to read and more likely to be read. Self-discipline is required, together with a rigorous adherence to priorities in order to edit out the least valuable material. Cutting marginal topics eases the reader's burden and detracts little, if at all, from the report's value. Inexperienced report writers may like to keep a record of what they eliminate from earlier drafts. It's astonishing how much you can lose without reducing the report's impact.

Keep the fog factor low

The fog factor is a score derived by calculating the average number of words of more than three syllables per sentence. The lower the fog factor, the less is demanded of the reader. If the fog factor is more than three and a half, there's a danger you'll encounter readership resistance. It takes humility to reduce the fog factor (we all love our long words), but it's even more humbling to discover that you've produced a report that nobody's reading.

Make the data talk

Data don't have a voice of their own. In a well-constructed table, patterns and exceptions are instantly obvious. Impact is more important than absolute accuracy, so prune numbers to the right of the decimal point ruthlessly, round up, order rows and columns by size, and give each table a short verbal summary.

These suggestions sound obvious. But it takes real application to use them when writing, because they're designed to aid the reader. If you get the story and structure right before you start, you shouldn't have too much painful editing to do later. Don't forget to allow time for redrafting, which may be easier for someone else to do. Never submit a report which hasn't been read for sense and for accessibility by at least one other person, preferably someone not involved in its creation.

When asked to make a presentation in support of a written report, it's fatal to assume your audience will have read it. Indeed, human nature being what it is, assume that they haven't. However, your presentation must not consist of a parrot-like repetition of the written version, because someone in the audience *will* have done their homework and they should be rewarded for their conscientiousness. Remember too that a bored listener is a potential mischief-maker.

Making presentations

The first rule of making presentations is simple: don't believe people who tell you you'll be able to think on your feet. Very few people can, and the consequences of standing up in front of an audience without knowing what you're going to say can be horrific. Not only must you know what you want to say, you should know enough about them to have a shrewd idea of what they expect to hear and what their reaction is likely to be. In order to make your case effectively, you must therefore:

- show that it is based on facts;

- spell out the benefits it offers to the organisation and to individual members of the audience;

- give an honest and realistic estimate of costs.

Almost everybody is nervous about speaking in public. If you feel no anxiety, you'll bore your audience rigid. Realising this, some professional speakers who have become blasé deliberately frighten themselves or run on the spot outside the conference room to get their adrenalin going! If your problem is too much rather than too little adrenalin, and you're worried you'll be too frightened to think, I can offer two reassuring observations.

1   The learning curve for public speaking is sharper than for almost any management activity I have studied. Most people improve dramatically over their first few presentations and everyone can benefit from training in presentation skills.

2   If you have prepared the subject thoroughly and keep reminding yourself that you know more about it than anyone in the audience, the two great anxieties of the public speaker – drying up and having your ignorance exposed – are greatly reduced. If you're a nervous speaker, you'll probably find all audiences equally threatening. In fact, however, research shows that audiences of strangers, and those containing your superiors, are actually less threatening than groups of your peers.

Here are some tips to increase your confidence as a public speaker.

●   *Check out the room beforehand*   Make sure you're familiar with the available facilities and the layout. And make sure you know how the technology works!

●   *Rehearse*   Rehearsing with an audience (one person will do) increases your confidence, helps you get the timing right and gives you a chance to hear feedback about any irritating verbal or visual mannerisms you have. Aim to achieve a happy medium between the zombie-like immobility of TV newsreaders and the distracting rubber limbs of Magnus Pyke. Variety should be your target, in how you look and how you sound. Alter your pace, volume and tone, and use your hands, for emphasis and to convey an air of relaxed control.

●   *Stand up*   It gives you more authority and will force you to remember that you are performing. It takes a real professional to keep an audience's attention when sitting down. When standing, be careful not to sway around too much. You can walk about, but pacing up and down is a distraction. Keep your hands out of your pockets, and try to look like somebody who's in control of the situation and enjoying themselves.

●   *Start powerfully*   A strong beginning is the key to an effective presentation. Set the scene, perhaps using a graphic image to illustrate the problem you are proposing to solve. Some speakers like to start quietly and gain attention by suddenly changing gear later. It's a risky ploy for the inexperienced speaker. Much safer to grab your audience's attention from the start and not let go until you've finished with them!

● *Structure your talk around the central theme*   The audience will appreciate it if you stick to one or two central themes and signpost any deviations you make. Give interim summaries and keep the continuity going. Construct an argument that leads to a positive, irresistible conclusion.

● *Three's enough!*   Having decided on your main message, follow the Rule of Three: most people can't absorb more than three new ideas in one sitting.

● *Illustrate key points with vivid examples and use visual aids*   Use real-life people and true stories to illustrate the different steps in your argument. This helps the audience to conjure up mental images which keep them interested now and help them remember what you have said later. You can't assume that your audience is going to take in more than one-third of what you say, so reinforce your message with visual aids.

● *Use cards*   Cue cards are the least obtrusive way of helping you to remember the sequence of your argument. Write a couple of main points on each, with three or four sub-headings. Don't use complete sentences – a few words is the most you can take in at a glance. It is quite a good idea, however, to write out your opening and closing remarks in full on separate cards. You can then learn these by heart, ensuring a confident start and a positive end to your presentation. Never read from a text or have sheets of notes!

● *Use short sentences*   Avoid going into too much detail. Be succinct and never talk for more than 40 minutes at a time. Twenty or 30 minutes is better.

- *Breathe deeply from your stomach, and don't forget to pause*   If you breathe from your throat you'll sound raspy and nervous. Rehearsing will show you where to pause – between the key points, which gives them a chance to sink in.

- *Make eye contact*   Your eyes are an important link with your audience. Look at them, try to assess their reaction and adjust to it. Locate some friendly faces at different points in the room and return to them regularly, to make sure you seem to be addressing everyone.

- *End with a strong message and image*   Work out in advance the message you want to leave your listeners with. It should be as powerful as your opening thrust and must reinforce your key point. A five-point action plan will reassure them there's a way to achieve what you're proposing – and that you know what it is!

Handling meetings

Relatively few meetings involve song-and-dance presentations. Most are mundane, bread-and-butter affairs, aimed to keep the everyday business of the organisation flowing smoothly. People make progress reports to colleagues, settle disputes that arose last month, announce what they hope to do next month and so on. But they are still places where things can be made to happen. Indeed, I think it's a characteristic of really successful operators that they treat regular meetings as invaluable sources of information and opportunities to rehearse their skills in handling meetings.

To make things happen, you have to be able to control a meeting effectively, i.e. ensure that it's conducted along lines that suit your purpose without participants feeling they are being manipulated. Here are some observations which may help you achieve this:

- people are more malleable when they are feeling good about being in a meeting;

- a meeting has failed if even one participant leaves feeling they have gained nothing from attending it;

- meetings are more likely to succeed if they are scheduled well in advance, have an agenda, start on time and follow prearranged time limits on each item, and if participants are allowed to suggest items for any other business at the beginning of the meeting, but not thereafter;

- the quality of regular meetings improves if they are regularly assessed for performance of the Chair, progress made, teamwork, clarity of objectives, level of participation, and ways of improving output;

- meetings tend to turn ugly when participants stop listening to each other, people are allowed to repeat themselves, raise irrelevant issues, or backtrack, people stop responding to the feelings their contribution is arousing, timings are allowed to drift, and decisions lack clarity.

The art of listening

Your success as a speaker in any context depends critically on your listening ability. You need to exploit your knowledge of the art of listening to make your audience listen to you. But it's just as important that you interpret accurately what you hear while researching your audience to make your case to them – or him or her, since some of your most important selling jobs will have an audience of only one!

There are seven important principles you need to follow to be a really effective listener.

- Stop talking, especially that internal, mental silent chatter – and answering back. Let the speaker finish. Hear them out. This is particularly important when you're in a thoroughly familiar situation. The temptation is to complete the speaker's sentence for them and work out a reply, assuming you know what they're going to say, instead of listening to what they are actually saying.

- Relax. Research shows that tension reduces the effectiveness of your auditory receptors. So a good listener must be relaxed.

- Put the speaker at ease by showing that you're listening. The good listener doesn't look over someone's shoulder or write while the speaker is talking. If you do have to take notes on what is being said, explain what you are doing. Blame your poor memory, and make it clear that your notetaking shows how important what they're saying is. You have to be careful here, because we all rely on the expression on another person's face to tell us how we are faring in a conversation. So people get nervous when the person they're talking to looks away or concentrates on what they're writing, instead of nodding reassuringly.

- Remember that your aim in listening is to understand what the speaker is saying, not to win an argument. That comes later!

- Be aware of your personal prejudices and make a conscious effort to stop them influencing your judgement. Don't make assumptions about the person talking on the basis that they have a beard, grey hair, short skirt or whatever.

- Listen with feeling as well as reason. Your main objective is to get inside the other person's head. What would you mean if you were saying what he or she is saying?

- Be alert to what the speaker is *not* saying, as well as what they are. Very often what's missing is more important than what's there. Again, ask yourself, what would it mean if you had left out what they have just failed to say?

To do your job properly, you'll need to spend at least half your time listening to what other people say. It's an active process, never more important than when you're meeting someone for the first time – when your objective should be to say as little and learn as much as possible in the shortest time.

Some people dismiss listening as an automatic process, while others regard it as an easily acquired skill. I don't think it's either. Nor do I think it's easy to get people to listen to you. Just think of all the things they can do instead. They may be:

- thinking about what to say back (rehearsing a reply);

- settling on some advice to give ('If I were you . . .');

- preparing a judgement ('You were absolutely right!' or 'Don't you think you were rather impatient?');

- worrying that you'll be upset by their reaction;

- feeling anxious that they can't think of any reply to what you're saying;

- impatient for you to finish, because
  —they don't agree with you,
  —they're just not interested,
  —they agree, but find what you're saying obvious;

- distracted by an episode in their own past that seems relevant ('Oh yes, this reminds me of that time on the M25!');

- distracted by something quite irrelevant that has somehow sprung into their mind ('My God! I forgot to turn the gas off!' or 'How on earth am I going to get back to Hitchin before the pub closes?').

So never take an audience's attention for granted, however rapt they may look. And if they're sitting with their chins down, arms folded across their chest and legs tightly crossed, you're in real trouble! In body language this means I don't like what I'm hearing and I'd much rather be somewhere else. Since psychologists calculate that two-thirds of communication happens non-verbally, it's a subject you'll need to study if you want to become a master of the art of listening. Look out for the raised steeple (two sets of fingers raised and touching each other in the shape of a steeple or wigwam) which conveys bored smugness, the hands tightly clasped behind the back which means that someone is about to lose their rag, and the shifty feet or quick stroke of the nose that indicates tension, embarrassment or even that someone is being economical with the truth.

Why do we get our wires crossed?

Communication is the process by which information is transmitted. Given the difficulties and distractions faced by communicators, and those on the receiving end, it's not surprising the process is so often flawed. There's a plethora of perils facing the would-be communicator. But you may find the following list of questions useful to help you identify some of the most common obstacles to effective communication.

The message

Is what I'm saying today relevant today? Is it appropriate and/or necessary? Is it really just yesterday's message? Or is it years ahead of its time? Is it just a bee in my bonnet? *Why* am I saying what I'm saying, in the way that I'm saying it, today?

The medium

Is the technology I'm using the ideal one for the message I'm trying to convey, or is it just a matter of expedience (what happened to be available, given that I didn't plan the presentation early enough to know what I really needed) or laziness on my part (this is how I've always done it)? Ought I to be looking at different media? What can I learn from other communicators?

The audience

Is it the right size? The right composition? Are some things best communicated in mixed function groups of the whole team, others to smaller groups, who speak the same technical language, share the same experiences and problems, and will therefore be more likely to gel as a group and help each other? But what about creative tension? How important is it to have people who can represent different perspectives?

The time and place

We all function better at some times of the day than at others. For example, two out of three people are at their best intellectually in the morning. The post-lunch dip (2 to 4 p.m.) is probably the worst time to schedule an important communication. Most people also find it easier to remember what they have learnt in the place where they originally learnt it. That's why the trend is towards training in the work environment instead of in a training centre.

The communicator

Ask yourself, am I . .

- overfamiliar with my material?

- insufficiently aware of the audience?

- concerned only with output, not input?

- unwilling to learn from others?

- lacking the imagination to judge the effect of my words?

- out of date or ignorant?

- giving a poorly planned presentation?

- failing to practise what I preach (e.g. giving an off-the-peg presentation, when I'm telling the audience how important it is to treat other people as individuals)?

- suffering from the gloating expert syndrome (i.e. enjoying the fact that I know more than the audience does and teasing them by withholding information that they would dearly love to have)?

Do you know how to negotiate?

Even the most effective communicator sometimes comes up against a brick wall. You've made your case as effectively as you know how, listened to all the objections, and responded sensitively to every nuance and hidden agenda item you could detect. But you can't shift them. They've got their view. It's incompatible with yours, and yet you have to live with each other. It's time to negotiate.

Traditionally, negotiation was regarded as a sort of battle, where one side's victories were the other's defeats. This 'Win-Lose' model is neither desirable nor appropriate in an organisation – or anywhere else where the two sets of negotiators are likely to meet again to resolve a different set of issues. The slate should be clean at the beginning of a negotiation, and this won't be the case if one side is still smarting from the defeat it suffered last time the two sides met. A good negotiation starts from the recognition that there is a clash between legitimate interests, but that everyone accepts that a solution must be found.

Negotiations take place in an atmosphere of uncertainty, with neither side knowing precisely what the other would be prepared to settle for. The events that make up the negotiation process tend to divide up into four different phases. Each calls for a different set of tactics, as you can see from the model below.

The Four Phases of Negotiation

Phase 1: Preparation

EVENTS

— Objectives set
— Data assembled
— Strategy decided

TACTICS

— Define your bargaining objective as follows:
— *ideal* – the best you can hope to achieve;
— *minimum* – the least you would be prepared to settle for;
— *target* – what you're going to try for, and have a realistic chance of achieving.

— Consider how you might build a package which would allow concessions to be exchanged

— Assess what the other party wants, or is prepared to offer

Phase 2: Opening

EVENTS
— Both sets of negotiators reveal their initial bargaining positions.

TACTICS

— Open realistically and move moderately

— Challenge the other party's position as it stands – but be careful not to force them into a corner
— Explore attitudes, ask questions, observe behaviour. Above all, assess the other party's strengths, weaknesses and tactics
— Don't make concessions

Phase 3: Bargaining

EVENTS

— Weaknesses in the other side's argument probed
— Attempt made to persuade them to abandon their position and move closer to yours
— Own position reassessed to check that it holds good in the light of the information given by the other side
— Pressure applied, concessions offered

TACTICS

— Always make conditional proposals – 'I'll do this if you consider doing that'
— Never make one-sided concessions
— Where possible, negotiate on the whole package. If it has to be broken down make sure it's you who does it – and don't allow the other party to pick you off item by item

Phase 4: Closing

EVENTS

— Judgement as to whether the other side is determined to stick to its position or will settle for a compromise
— Final trade-offs
— Settlement

TACTICS

— Offer a minor concession, in return for agreement to settle
— Do the deal, perhaps by splitting the difference or introducing an entirely new element
— Summarise what has happened, emphasising the concessions you've made and that this really is your final position.

The negotiation process has a language all of its own. Inexperienced negotiators can be baffled by the contradictions between what's said and what actually happens. Here is a translation of some of the commonest examples of Negotiatorspeak.

WHAT THEY SAY	WHAT THEY MEAN
That's as far as I can go	I might be able to persuade my boss to go further
We don't usually give more than 5 per cent discount	We'd be prepared to give more if you offered us something in return
Let's just think about that	I'm prepared to negotiate
It will be very difficult for us to meet that requirement	It's not impossible but we'd be looking for a trade off
I shall certainly consider your offer	I'm going to accept it but I don't want to seem an easy touch
This is our standard contract	We're prepared to negotiate terms of business
We are prepared to offer you £x per y units	The price is negotiable
That is my final offer	My boss might go even further if pushed
We couldn't meet your delivery requirements at that price	We'll negotiate on delivery price

What do you do when things don't happen?

You ask yourself two questions: why isn't it happening; and is there anything I can do about it? One possibility is that you've simply run out of steam. Some people complain that the implementation phase of a project lacks the glamour of the creative planning stage. So you have to be prepared for the sense of anticlimax and ready to gee your team up through the period of post-natal depression. Your brainchild needs to be kept alive until it develops a life of its own.

The second possibility is that you've run into a wall of conservatism. People accept what you're recommending intellectually, but are resistant emotionally to the consequences of implementing your programme. Change is an emotional issue. People are required to abandon the habits of a lifetime. Often it's trivial details that cause the most trouble – shifting a couple of plants, or adding an extra responsibility that won't take more than five minutes a day. But people grow attached to their own way of doing things. ('It may not be a particularly good habit, but at least it's mine!'). People get scared as they think through the implications of a change programme. Some of the changes seem inconceivable: surely that could never work (but it already does, at your major competitor's place!)? They worry that the change process will be unpredictable, at times irrational. They're right: it will be.

Your job is to reassure them that although your proposal is difficult, it's do-able – and must be done. So their best policy is to get comfortable with the new ideas rather than fight them. The process of change is in fact much less threatening now than it was 25 years ago. So much more is now known about what happens in organisations when they change that there's really no need for alarm – or much excuse for failure.

It's a question of everyone being asked to make small adjustments, rather than a few people undertaking massive change. Because so many people are involved, you have to make allowances for the fact that they'll change at different rates, depending upon their style of learning, personality and motivation. Broadly speaking, the better someone is performing today, the more efficient they will be at picking up new ways of doing things tomorrow. We know that change tends to take longer than your most wildly pessimistic estimate. You can expect a company-wide initiative to take about a year and a half to bite and perhaps twice as long to impact on the bottom line, though you'd hope to register perceptible successes sooner than this – ideally, within a couple of months of the programme getting underway.

However many people are involved, the basic change unit is always the same size: one. Change is introduced in an organisation, however large, by convincing individuals that it's necessary and can be done. The organisation changes when the number of individuals converted reaches a critical mass. So it's crucial to explain to people why they're being asked to change. They should also be offered a choice as to how they will shape their contribution to the agreed corporate goal. Although change can only happen at an individual level, how one person works is bound to have an impact on people around them. So you have to give advance warning of particular changes, not just to those who are carrying them out, but to everyone affected by those people. The most powerful conclusion that emerges from all this research is that most people aren't opposed to the idea of change at all – only to the methods that can be used to introduce it.

Thanks to the efforts of the media, most people today understand very well the need for change. If they're thoughtful, they'll be more worried if their organisation is not reviewing its way of doing things! But they do want to be consulted. It's not enough just to tell them what's happening. They need to be involved in the detailed planning, where they are affected. Understand and act on all of this, and you may find that suddenly things are happening after all!

But don't get complacent as you see resistance melting. People need help through the process of change. Specifically they need:

● information (I know what's going on);

● involvement (I'm part of this);

● support and reassurance (I can play my part, and it's an important one);

● guidance (I know what I'm meant to be doing);

● easy access to the person in charge (they value my opinion);

● an opportunity to discuss how the process is affecting them (they care about me);

● clarification (they don't give me nasty surprises);

● respect for values and dignity (I haven't been made to give up anything that's really important to me);

● hope (I know it's worth it – and we can do it!).

So much for the management of change in organisations. We shall have more to say about how you can help people prepare themselves for change in Chapter 6.

A final reason why things don't happen is a serious one – the conflict of ideas or personalities. There's always conflict in organisations, even when not much is happening. People's objectives, values and needs don't always coincide. Nor is conflict always a bad thing. It tends to have negative connotations of argument, disagreement, even physical violence. But disagreement doesn't have to be disagreeable, and dispute can be confined to principles rather than personalities. It's also worth recalling Richard Pascale's sobering conclusion when he revisited the companies singled out for their excellence by Tom Peters only five years earlier. Two-thirds of them had slipped from their pinnacle, largely as a result of complacency. They had become too coherent and too successful at outlawing conflict.

Conflict is usually counter-productive when it stems from a personality clash or when you allow it to become so. What happens is much less important than the effect produced. People can come to blows, or lie on the floor kicking and screaming, without any long-term damage being caused. Indeed, a good temper tantrum can even unblock the situation or trigger off a conceptual breakthrough – provided it happens at the right time. But you do have to understand how to cope with conflict. There are three alternatives.

- Avoid the issue, by minimising the problem, procrastinating or dealing with the symptoms of conflict rather than its causes.

- Square up to each other. Don't give an inch – and keep your powder dry!

- Try to resolve the conflict.

In the short term, you can pussyfoot around with the first two alternatives. Eventually, however, the conflict will have to be resolved – not just to make things happen, but in the interest of organisational harmony. Once again there are three alternatives.

- *Peaceful co-existence*   The aim here is to reformulate the problem, playing down the differences and emphasising the common ground. This is more applicable to personality clashes, though even here it's an uneasy solution. False *bonhomie* doesn't last, and the real issues will probably surface again.

- *Compromise*   A 'Win–Win' negotiation (following the rules outlined earlier where neither side feels that they've lost) appeals to pragmatists more than to idealists. The assumption is that there's no best solution – an idea committed managers may find hard to swallow – and once again the real issues have not been resolved.

- *Genuine resolution*   Using the problem-solving methods outlined in Chapter 4, you try to find a genuine solution to the problem, rather than merely accommodating conflicting points of view. The atmosphere of conflict and tension can be exploited to galvanise people into thinking again, trying fresh approaches, considering new ideas and creating a new dynamic of co-operation and discussion.

That's the optimistic view. In the real world, you may still be in deep trouble, confronted by obstacles. At such a late stage in the proceedings, this can constitute a crisis in your campaign to make things happen. As in all crises, it's essential to keep cool and maintain the confidence of those around you. It can be helpful to give the impression that you are relaxed about things when in fact your brain is in overdrive (but remember what happened to Prime Minister James 'Crisis, what crisis?' Callaghan). You'll need all the decision-making skills discussed in Chapter 4, not just to keep your show on the road, but also to inspire your team. But ignore that treacherous little voice urging you to do something immediately! The process of crisis management starts with containment, and you need to buy time to prepare contingency plans. Here are 10 suggestions for managers confronted by crisis.

1   Don't suppress panic – but keep it to yourself!
2   Line up a trusted confidant/sounding board – you're going to need one.
3   Load shed (i.e. get rid of peripheral problems) and relegate items that have no bearing on the crisis to the back burner.
4   Adopt 'helicopter vision' to make an assessment of the situation. Imagine yourself looking down on the scene and ask yourself these questions.

What's really happening?

Why's it happening?

What will actually happen if I don't do anything?

How quickly do I need to act to stop the damage spreading?

Who else is involved?

Who's likely to become involved?

What resources have I got – people, equipment, finance, back-up from other organisations?

Has anything like this happened before that I can learn from?

5   Select a team to deal with the situation. Allocate roles and tasks, and establish authority to act. Remember that the leader's finger needs to be on the pulse during a crisis.

6   Set up a communication system which tells you exactly what's happening, and gives you immediate access to the whole team.

7   Draw up your preliminary step-by-step plan of action. Prepare other contingency plans. Invite input from key members of the team.

8   Prepare your detailed plans. They should include time scales, scope for cooling-off period, longer-term solutions and fine-tuned contingency plans.

9   Monitor continually precisely what is happening. Ensure that you get the information you need fast, so you can react rapidly but not irresponsibly.

10   Evaluate actions and reactions constantly. You'll need to modify the plan as events unfold and take swift corrective steps.

If the thinking behind your proposal was sound, and your strategy and tactics well prepared and executed, the chances are you will make it happen. There's a favourable wind for change in organisations today, and people may even be grateful to you for showing them the way forward, provided you do it sensitively and sell your ideas effectively.

That said, you won't win 'em all. Sometimes you'll have to accept that you've backed a loser. In which case, put a brave face on it and head for the refreshment tent. But don't sulk. People dislike bad losers even more than they dislike losers. You'll be back. On other occasions, the issue won't be quite so clear-cut. Sometimes 'No' doesn't mean 'Never', but just 'Not today'. Or it may even mean 'Not the way you're suggesting' – a tacit invitation to try again.

Winners can see a sliver of silver in even the darkest cloud, and detect opportunities where others see only obstacles. As they back out of the boardroom smiling gamely, they know they're going to make it happen – next time.

Chapter 6

Walking the Tightrope

Managing effectively is a demanding task. It's also draining. You have to give a lot of yourself – to the organisation, to your own work and to your people. The danger is that there's not enough left for yourself or for the people who are important to you in other areas of life. There are three main risks:

- you get ground down by the pressures of everyday working life;

- the different parts of your life get out of balance, with the scales tilting too heavily towards work;

- you become so involved in what's happening today that you fail to plan for tomorrow.

The committed manager is like an apprentice tightrope walker, still uncertain how much concentration it takes to avoid a fall. Here are five questions that need to be answered.

1   Where does the stress come from and what should you do with it?
2   How can you balance your life successfully?
3   Can you have your cake and eat it?
4   How should you handle Crazy Time?
5   How will you manage tomorrow?

Where does the stress come from and what should you do with it?

The pace of life is increasingly relentless. New things happen more often. We travel greater distances more quickly. Messages can be sent and action expected at shorter and shorter intervals. We are bombarded with events which force us to recognise, confront and adapt to change. This offers us enormous benefits. Human beings are born inquisitive, and thrive on new discoveries. We raise our targets and increase our achievements each time we manage a change successfully – and we learn valuable lessons for bigger challenges in the future when we understand mistakes we have made in the past.

But there's a price to be paid for all this – stress. By definition a stressor is anything which forces you to adapt or change in order to cope with a new situation. Each new challenge represents a problem which needs to be solved – and if it isn't, the result can be stress. This doesn't mean that all the challenges are stressors. But they have the potential to be – if there's a mismatch between the challenge and how you believe you can deal with it, or you haven't the freedom to solve the problem as you'd like, or you're short of sources of help, advice and understanding.

A recent survey of some of Europe's top chief executives confirms that stress isn't confined to middle management. UMIST's School of Management found that work stress often made 23 per cent of the executives polled consider leaving their jobs. Many of them felt they did not spend enough time with their families, with 45 per cent saying that work made unreasonable demands on their relationship with their family, and 48 per cent finding that work intruded into their private and family life. We shall return to his theme later in the chapter.

Stress is widely known for its impact on physical health – but significant changes in feelings, reactions and behaviour are just as important. Its effects are as far-reaching as its sources are wide, affecting how you live your life inside and outside work. Stress can be the reason why problems don't get resolved. Minor illnesses linger, days in bed lead inevitably to a build-up of work, and a vicious spiral is established. It all leads towards the dreadful feeling that there's so much to do you don't know where to start – so you don't. You may not be able to escape the pressures and tensions of everyday life, but being aware of the origins of stress and how it affects you personally are important first steps in reducing and controlling the impact it has on you.

Different people are affected by stress in different ways and to different extents. Understanding these individual differences is, as always, the key. It is also important to recognise that stress is not necessarily an evil. It can be the force which holds you together when the going gets really tough. But you have to recognise your optimum stress level for performance – exceeding this is where the danger lies.

Almost anything can become a source of pressure – especially at work. Think about your job and see whether you are affected by any of the following.

		YES	NO
1	*Far too much to do*	☐	☐
2	*Not enough influence over what needs to be done*	☐	☐
3	*The people I manage are too demanding*	☐	☐
4	*Not enough support from above*	☐	☐
5	*Too many new ideas to cope with*	☐	☐
6	*People don't back me up*	☐	☐
7	*My job pulls me in too many different directions at once*	☐	☐
8	*They're always moving the goalposts*	☐	☐
9	*Having to deal with 'difficult' situations*	☐	☐
10	*Personality clashes with colleagues*	☐	☐

Give yourself a point for every 'Yes' box you've ticked. The higher your score, the more sources of pressure you have in your job. If you've scored more than four, take a hard look at the way you handle your job. Which are the pressure points you've identified? Should you be looking for more control over the way you operate or asking people for more support? Do you need to rethink the way you organise your time?

All managers experience pressure in their jobs. Are you clear about the difference between pressures which constitute a challenge and those which create stress? It's up to you to know yourself sufficiently well to recognise the point at which your performance and health are suffering. You can push your personal boundaries back – research shows that the more stress you have to deal with, the more resilient you become. So it's worth pushing your limits – but not to the detriment of your health or performance.

In Chapter 2, I suggested that all management tasks are aimed at one of three goals: survival, maintenance and development. This analysis can also be applied to managers. *Surviving* means keeping going in the face of difficult circumstances, shocks or crisis. You can probably remember a time when you had to fight hard to survive. *Maintenance* refers to the kind of bread and butter activities you have to perform to keep things ticking over from one week to the next. *Development* refers to a real change in the sort of person that you are and the way you operate. Development often results from crisis. Senior managers regard a time of crisis as an ideal opportunity to assess real managerial quality. You should be no less interested to use it to put your own strengths and weaknesses to the test.

It's vital to have strategies to cope with the pressures that are part of every manager's life. Here is a list of the main sources of stress at work:

- tasks which are too demanding/undemanding;

- lack of power or influence;

- conflict between personal and organisational values;

- role ambiguity;

- responsibility without control;

- relationships with colleagues;

- dissatisfaction with career and achievement;

- organisational structure and climate;

- time constraints;

- lack of necessary skills;

- reliance on outside agencies;

- high concentration/low stimulation;

- over-demanding targets.

How well equipped are you to cope with these threats? You can assess your armoury of stress beaters by deciding which of the following statements apply to you.

		TRUE	FALSE
1	*I try to be realistic about what I can and cannot achieve.*	☐	☐
2	*I'm usually hesitant about approaching senior managers for advice and support.*	☐	☐
3	*I can't say I have any particular hobbies or pastimes.*	☐	☐
4	*Compared with most people I manage my time at work pretty well.*	☐	☐
5	*My home isn't really a refuge – it's just somewhere to sleep at night.*	☐	☐
6	*If I have a set of different problems I usually find it difficult to concentrate on one in particular.*	☐	☐
7	*I find the best way to deal with a difficult situation is to stand back and really think things through.*	☐	☐
8	*I'm not very good at delegating.*	☐	☐
9	*As soon as a problem rears its head, I start trying to deal with it.*	☐	☐
10	*I try to find ways of varying my work to make it more interesting.*	☐	☐

Give yourself one point for each 'False' box you have ticked for questions 1, 4, 7, 9 and 10, and one point for every 'True' box you have ticked for questions 2, 3, 5, 6 and 8. The higher your score, the less able you are to cope with the effects of stress. If you have scored more than 3 points, I think you should take active steps to increase your range of coping techniques.

If stress is a state that arises from not being able to solve problems, coping with stress has to involve ways of making the task of problem-solving easier. There are two ways of going about this.

Problem-solving strategies

You can remove the source of the problem by reducing the number of problems created and by allowing more time to solve those created by other people. You can do this by learning to solve problems system-atically and by managing your activities, time and resources more effectively. Your problem-solving arsenal for stress reduction should include:

- time management;

- problem-solving and decision-making;

- setting goals;

- self-appraisal.

Personal strategies

The positive approach is to employ a series of behavioural techniques, for example physical exercise, assertiveness and relaxation training. The negative approach concentrates on dulling your senses. Alcohol in small doses can be an effective painkiller. Tranquillisers are not recommended, except as a very short-term measure. They prevent the development of the natural toughening-up process and are therefore counter-productive as stress reducers if used more than once or twice in quick succession.

Always remember, though, that stress in manageable doses is a positive force. It gees you up, and without it you'd find it very difficult to perform. To benefit from stress, you need to be aware of your own peak stress levels and learn how not to exceed them. By keeping the following in mind, you'll use your natural coping mechanisms to best advantage:

- anticipate and avoid situations which overload you with stress;

- step back from difficult situations and look at exactly why they are stressful – learn some lessons for the future;

- alter your perception of events – look at stressful situations as challenging opportunities for problem-solving;

- be aware of negative emotions, such as harbouring grudges – against yourself or other people – and try to get rid of them;

- always seek to improve your physical health by making an effort to exercise regularly and learning a relaxation technique that suits you.

How can you balance your life successfully?

All the evidence suggests that being able to cope successfully with the demands of your job makes an enormous contribution to your psychological well-being. But it isn't the whole story. There's another side of life, which usually involves family and leisure interests. Most people's vision of personal success includes finding a satisfactory balance between work and the rest of life.

You have to make a trade-off between home and work, between the demands of private and professional life, and between personal relationships and professional commitments. Some people believe that success at work can only be achieved by making sacrifices in other areas. Their thinking goes as follows: 'I only have a finite amount of energy. So the more I devote to work, the less there is for the rest of life. Therefore, the more successful I am at work, the less likely I am to make a success of my personal life.'

It's a worrying train of thought, and I want to try to persuade you that it doesn't have to be like this. You can have the best of both worlds, provided you follow some simple rules and acquire some basic life skills. Specifically, you have to understand the importance of planning and timing, to be comfortable with the change process, to understand how other people operate, and understand yourself quite well, too. To see how well you're managing the balancing act at present, read through the following statements and say whether or not they apply to you.

		TRUE	FALSE
1	*I often go through an entire weekend without spending any time on work brought home from the office.*	☐	☐
2	*Events at work sometimes force me to miss occasions at home which my family have particularly asked me to get back for.*	☐	☐
3	*I never dream about work problems.*	☐	☐
4	*I have at least three significant leisure interests that have nothing to do with my work.*	☐	☐
5	*When I am ill, I tend to take work to bed with me.*	☐	☐
6	*I find it easier to talk to work colleagues than to my partner or friends.*	☐	☐

	TRUE	FALSE
7 *It is very unusual for me to ring home to say I'm going to be back later than planned.*	☐	☐
8 *I have had to cancel at least one holiday due to pressure of work.*	☐	☐
9 *When I'm trying to read a book or magazine, I find my mind keeps wandering back to work problems.*	☐	☐
10 *I find it a relief to meet new people who have nothing whatever to do with my line of business.*	☐	☐

Score two points for every 'True' answer to statements 1, 3, 4, 7 and 10, and zero points for every 'False' response. For statements 2, 5, 6, 8 and 9, score two points for each 'False' reply, and zero points for every 'True'. A score of 16 or more suggests that you have managed to achieve a healthy balance between your professional and private life. It's not that you are not fully committed to your job, just that you recognise that the price of professional success does not have to be failure in other areas of life. A score of 12–14 suggests that when office and domestic or leisure interests come into conflict, work comes first. Improving your performance in the office would reduce the number of occasions when you feel forced to disappoint your family and friends. A score of 10 or less points to workaholism. For you, life outside the office hardly counts.

Workaholism is a frame of mind which can threaten your well-being and the happiness of those who care for you. Workaholics come in two varieties. First, there are those people whose work is never done. Surrounded by files and papers, they feel they can never take a breathing space. At weekends, they feel guilty unless they are in the office or at home with a briefcase full of work. The second type of workaholic simply loves their work. They're totally enthusiastic about what they do and can't think of a better way to spend their time. These two different types of manager have been dubbed 'drudges' and 'dynamos', and there's a vast difference between being driven by obsession (drudges) and by enthusiasm (dynamos).

There's another useful distinction to be drawn. 'Outer-directed' managers are motivated primarily by money, power or the pursuit of security. 'Inner-directed' managers, by contrast, do what they do out of conviction and commitment. They have vision and often possess considerable personal charisma. I shall argue later that, in future, it is inner-directed managers who are more likely to feel at ease. At present, however, only a minority of managers appear to fit this pattern.

Many managers fail to master the juggling act between domestic and professional commitments. Let me tell you about the results of the largest survey ever carried out to investigate managers' priorities and values. Four out of 5 of those questioned said they valued their home life at least as much as their work. Less than 1 in 10 put career solely as top value. The majority, however, agreed that they looked for different things from their families and their jobs.

Generally speaking, people with families seem to regard them as the most important aspect of their lives, though they admit that they get the greatest sense of achievement and mastery from work. However, nearly half of those surveyed said that they were dissatisfied with the way they distributed their time and energy. For all your good intentions, I imagine that most people reading this book will probably admit that work takes the lion's share of their energy. If you are like the people in the survey, almost half of you will add that you are dissatisfied with your current balance of priorities.

There will be many demands on you in the time you spend away from work. Families are certainly the most important one for most people, but many people also have leisure interests to which they are seriously committed. Your leisure interests can offer important clues as to how your professional and domestic lives are going. There are four different concepts of leisure:

- *Leisure as recovery* For example, watching TV, drinking, gardening or doing things around the house. There's not much conversation in this sort of leisure, and it's a pattern which often shows a high emotional spill-over (see below).

- *Leisure as relaxation* Unlike some other professional groups, managers spend a lot of time on sports and very active hobbies, such as squash, skiing and competitive tennis. These are satisfying outlets for tension and aggression, and may reduce stress, as stressing one system helps to relax another. That's why active sport can be more effective than simple rest.

146

- *Leisure as an investment in private life*   Leisure activities which involve the whole family represent a real investment in the family. They offer the prospect of a return on that investment, if it works out. There's some evidence that satisfaction in a marriage is linked to how much time the partners spend in joint leisure activities.

- *Leisure as personal development*   For some people, leisure provides an alternative career. It may be a question of some consuming passion like local politics or playing in an orchestra. This sort of leisure activity usually demands skills and expertise, and is more characteristic of later life.

Now for the downside! More than half the managers interviewed in the study said they see leisure as a source of conflict within the family. Again, it's a matter of decisions having to be made. Should leisure time be spent at home with the family or out on the tennis court? For a supportive partner, it's a cruel blow to find that your other half prefers to spend their limited time away from work without you. So – an active leisure life is not an automatic recipe for a happy home life!

When people are asked about the relationship between their personal and professional lives, four different patterns emerge. See which of them you recognise.

Pattern 1

Work and home exist side by side, independently.

Pattern 2

Work and home life are in direct conflict. You find it impossible to reconcile the demands of the two.

Pattern 3

One of the two (i.e. work or play) is simply a means to obtain something desirable in the other. You can either be one of those people who say the only reason they work is to get money to sustain their family, or you could be using one to make up for what is missing in the other. The workaholic may well have an emotional vacuum in the rest of their life, just as some people live through their family to an unhealthy extent, to compensate for disappointment at work.

Pattern 4

This pattern is known as 'crossed wires': what happens in one area of life has a spill-over effect on the other. Almost 60 per cent of managers describe the relationship between the two halves of their lives in this way. The spill-over can take different forms. It may be physical: for example, you're so exhausted when you get home that all you want to do is have a meal and go to sleep. Or you could be one of those people who gets so caught up in the 'tough guy' aspects of their role at work, that they find it impossible to be pleasant to their partner when they get home. Finally, you can become so dissatisfied with your job that you go into a decline which affects all aspects of life. Emotional spill-over from work is bound to affect the amount of energy you have left for your private life. This can work in either direction—making you extraordinarily bouncy or totally depressed.

Although work worries often spill over into private life, it's less common for private worries to interfere with how people perform at their job. Some managers pride themselves on their ability to look as though they're listening to their loved ones, while actually re-calculating monthly sales targets. Research suggests that 40 per cent of partners of successful executives believe that tension at work has a more damaging effect on how their partner behaves at home than anything else, including travelling. Here's a typical comment: 'I don't mind the amount of work he has to do, providing he's happy. What I do resent is the unhappiness he brings home.'

Can you have your cake and eat it?

So much for the bad news. However, the main conclusions of the study I have been quoting are surprisingly optimistic. Looking at all the evidence, the researchers suggest that, contrary to popular belief, professional and private life can actually complement and reinforce each other, rather than being antagonistic. The reason is very simple: both are enhanced by the same personal qualities and skills.

For example, communication skills are vital at work, but perhaps are more safely examined within the context of an intimate relationship. Other skills, acquired at work, may transfer effectively to the domestic area. For example, most managers are familiar with the benefits of working towards specific targets at work. It may not have occurred to them to work towards definite goals with their family. You might consider making a commitment to spend a certain amount of time playing with your children each weekend, or perhaps make a resolution to take up a new hobby or sport, and build it into your weekly programme. All you have to do is decide in detail what needs to be done, and you have a yardstick by which to measure success. See how your nearest and dearest respond to management by objectives!

Success in this sort of domestic project can create a spiral of self-confidence that spills over into professional life, which is why success in one area really can go hand in hand with success in the other. There are three skills which, taken together, increase the chances of success in both areas, and make it more likely that you'll be able to have your cake and eat it. By a happy chance, they are three of the major themes that we have already pursued together throughout this book. The first is the ability to get inside someone else's head to work out what they are thinking. The second is to be acutely aware of your own strengths and weaknesses, so that you can exploit the former and make allowances for the latter. The third is to be able to live comfortably with innovation and know how to rise to the challenge of change.

How should you handle Crazy Time?

In Chapter 4 we looked briefly at how change affects organisations. Recent research casts doubt on the effectiveness of traditional change programmes. The old-fashioned approach involved a company-wide initiative, led from the top, designed to alter formal structures and systems by attacking outmoded attitudes and skills. The most successful organisational change programmes have been quite different. They have usually started at the periphery of organisations, in an individual factory or site. They have been led by general managers or their equivalent, and they've achieved their results largely by finding new roles and responsibilities for people. The role of senior management has been confined to creating an environment which spawns such initiatives, nurtures them, tolerates their failures and publicises their successes across the whole organisation.

A well-designed change programme should begin with a diagnosis phase involving people in all parts and at all levels of the company. A new 'task-aligned' vision is created, and new roles and responsibilities emerge within existing functions, and – very importantly – in the interstices between departments. Every effort is made to achieve consensus, but people who, for whatever reason, are unable to come on board, are helped as humanely as possible out of the organisation. The message tends to spread horizontally rather than vertically, and whenever a change is successfully accomplished, it's immediately built into the system. The programme is continually monitored and fine-tuning occurs in response to what actually happens, rather than what was planned to happen. In other words, the programme is evolutionary and organic.

However well-designed the programme may be, real change is never painless. You can see where you are today and have a pretty clear idea of where you want to be in the future, but the period in between tends to be an uncomfortable experience. Some people call it Crazy Time, when the values of the old culture are still operating and those of the new have yet to prove their worth. As a manager, you have to help your people to get Crazy Time over as quickly and as painlessly as possible. You'll need to show vision and commitment, and you must expect to become emotionally involved with people who are finding it a struggle. You must practise what you preach, and your prowess as coach and mentor will be put to the test.

The change manager's task is to provide both castle and battlefield. Before you send your troops over the top, you have to gee them up for the fight. You should warn them they're going to be exposed to conflict, confrontation, stress and challenge – and there is no alternative. Back in the castle, however, you offer the troops access to all the relevant antidotes: support; validation ('Yes, what you're doing *is* right'); protection; and affirmation ('We *do* value your contribution!') – and you allow them to choose how they can contribute most effectively. Most managers are more comfortable with the supportive role. Some, however, get carried away by the military metaphors and become almost addicted to the change process. These 'change junkies' are the kind of managers who give the process a bad name. Change is certainly necessary in a changing world, but should never be introduced for its own sake.

But how can people learn to live with change and to thrive on the opportunities it creates? The first move is to get rid of four popular misconceptions.

● *Change can happen quickly*   It is tempting to hope for a quick solution once you have identified a problem. However, a process that involves changing people's life-long habits doesn't happen overnight. It's vital to avoid the mistake of aborting new programmes which are on the verge of working.

● *Resistance is worrying*   On the contrary, it's when everything is going too smoothly that a change specialist becomes suspicious. Resistance is inevitable, as people question methods and evaluate what they are being asked to do. If they say they're enjoying the process in the early stages, you'd be wise to assume that they've found some way round it and aren't really changing at all!

● *Solutions have to be perfect*   This is the classic civil service attitude – it's a delaying tactic designed to resist progress. If you wait until you have a perfect, all-embracing strategy, nothing will ever get done. In a change programme, you must expect to take the occasional step backwards in order to take two forwards. Minor setbacks don't matter – provided you're going in the right general direction. If the main enemy of change is giving up too soon, the second most formidable opponent has to be never getting started in the first place!

● *People can't change*   This is the most damaging assumption of all. The psychology of management is full of examples of leopards changing their spots and people transforming their fortunes by taking responsibility for their own lives. I'm not saying that it's easy, but I've seen it happen too many times to have any doubts that it can be done.

One way to make it easier is to tell people what happens to human beings as they change. Researchers have found that there are six stages through which everyone must expect to pass whenever they experience any form of significant change in their lives. Most of the research has involved people in new jobs or those who have to acquire new ways of working, but it's a general model of human behaviour that applies equally when you move house or start a new relationship. The six stages are universal and inevitable: no one will change without experiencing them.

Stage 1 The honeymoon

An initial period of euphoria lasts until you remember that there's no such thing as a free lunch! They may have offered you more money or a new job title, but there's always a *quid pro quo* required, e.g more commitment, more responsibility or the need to master new ways of doing things.

Stage 2 Identity crisis

Now you start asking yourself uncomfortable questions. Expect to hear yourself asking: 'What do they want from me?', 'Am I really up the job?', or 'What was wrong with the old way of doing things?'.

Stage 3 Incompetence

Suddenly, you notice that silly mistakes are creeping into your work. Tasks you've carried out perfectly without thinking for years are suddenly proving beyond you. The problem is that you're so wrapped up with your new responsibilities that you have no attention left for anything else. This stage can last for some while, and it may overlap with the next one.

Stage 4 Further questioning

Now your self-questioning becomes really searching: 'Why is nobody telling me what to do any more?', 'Where has all the support gone?', 'Who's supposed to be making the decisions round here? What do you mean, *I* am?'. Change these days tends to mean more responsibility and less reliance on other people. Becoming truly empowered isn't all a bed of roses. By Stage 4, you won't need to be reminded that change is never a painless process.

Stage 5 The trough

The trough is a state of mind, unpleasant and debilitating. It really does feel like you're trying to keep afloat in a sea of mud. You're floundering about, unable to think properly or to see a way out. The most difficult thing to accept about the trough is that you have to get yourself out of it. Other people – fellow swimmers or those standing on the outside – can offer advice, but only you can lever yourself out. There used to be two possibilities. The first was to give up and make for an organisation where the game was still played according to the old rules. That's not possible these days, because organisations are all dancing to the same tune, dictated by the same market conditions, and those that haven't learnt the new rules have almost all gone to the wall. The only way out of the trough now is to work out what's causing the pain. You must analyse your strengths in order to discover what adjustments have to be made to fit into the new environment. You need to prescribe a course of remedial action for yourself and follow it.

Stage 6 Back from the dead

The technical name for this stage is 'complete integration'. Slowly, you regain the old competence and with it, confidence returns. Now you're operating according to the new rules and feeling good about yourself for having made it.

Not everyone reaches Stage 6 in all change programmes, and it's not possible to say how long it takes to get through any of the stages. It depends on your capacity for taking on board new ways of doing things, and on the nature of the change involved. The only thing that's certain is that you won't be allowed to spend too long enjoying your success in Stage 6. They'll be back with the next set of changes, and there's you – back at Stage 1! But you'll probably recognise all these stages, now that they've been pointed out, and I hope that you'll be relieved to discover that what you may have thought of as personal weakness (or even symptoms of a mild nervous breakdown!) is in fact no more than the normal process of adjustment to altered circumstances. I can also reassure you that you meet an awfully nice class of manager in the trough!

How will you manage in tomorrow's world?

In Chapter 2, I said that effective managers need to possess 'helicopter vision' – the ability to position themselves above the fray, to look down on the whole battlefield, distinguish the wood from the trees, or whatever metaphor seems most appropriate! You need effective hindsight, too, to make sure that the lessons of yesterday are heeded and acted upon. But you also need foresight. You can't know exactly what is going to happen in the future, but you still have to look ahead, construct a series of plausible futures and try to prepare yourself for the most likely eventualities. As part of this exercise, you also need to make a cool assessment about the skills you are likely to need in order to survive and thrive in tomorrow's world, and to do everything in your power to make sure that you possess them before it arrives.

Let me turn now to my crystal ball, and make three predictions about the world of work at the end of the twentieth century. All have implications for the ambitious manager of today. First, markets will become even more global. As a result, the most successful organisations will be those in which local operators are equipped to make important decisions very rapidly – and certainly without time to consult the centre. Even relatively junior people will need to possess considerable business acumen and understand everything they need to know in order to make very significant business decisions – and get them right. Secondly, the importance of information and the speed with which it's transmitted will continue to increase. As a result, organisations will need a growing number of sophisticated analysts, planners and operators. Again, this suggests that cleverness, flexibility and courage will continue to be at a premium. Thirdly, and ironically, socio-demographic trends are such that the pool of skilled people may well be smaller rather than larger than it is today, which offers a great opportunity for those who consider themselves disadvantaged in today's world of work.

Your first glance at this vision of tomorrow's world may suggest that it will be big, fast and frightening. Paradoxically, however, I think that on closer investigation you may see it as quite the reverse. Because decision-making is going to become increasingly decentralised, small will become more beautiful. Things may be fast, but I don't think they will be furious. On the contrary, the stakes are going to be so high, and the risk factor so much greater, that the careful planning and development of human resources will be absolutely vital. I also think that as we come to understand more about managing change, and become more sophisticated in our approach to managing people generally, many of the causes of stress and anxiety in today's world of work will be brought under more effective control.

Finally, changes in the workplace have already made the concept of a job for life a thing of the past. It will become commonplace to have two or more careers in a working lifetime, and unusual not to shift employers frequently, and make the move between employment and self-employment several times. As a result, responsibility for career planning has to shift from personnel departments to individuals and their managers. The concept of a portable pension is already well accepted. The concept of a portable career is more challenging, but it's one that ambitious managers should be starting to get their minds round now.

So – what recipe am I recommending for success in tomorrow's world of work? So far as organisations are concerned, I can't improve on Tom Peters's eight point plan for survival. Tomorrow's successful organisation will offer: value; flexibility; quality; service; effectiveness; innovation; people-orientation; and leadership.

For individual managers, accountability and personal responsibility will be crucial determinants of success. To manage your people effectively, the virtues required in tomorrow's world won't be very different from those needed today, namely empathy, judgement, sensitivity, fairness and generosity. To help people change, you'll need vision, flexibility and the ability to cope with innovation, risks and failure. As for yourself, I think you'll need to be self-starting, self-determining and self-seeking. And I hope that this book will have helped you make substantial progress in all three directions.

Further reading

Adair, John, *Effective Teambuilding* (Gower, Hants, 1986).

Argyle, Michael and Trower, Peter, *Person to Person* (Harper and Row, London 1979).

Armstrong, Michael, *How to be an Even Better Manager* (Kogan Page Limited, London, 1988).

Armstrong, Michael, *A Handbook of Management Techniques* (Guild Publishing, London, 1986).

Belbin, Meredith, *Management Teams* (Heinemann, London, 1981).

Brown, Paul and Hackett, Fiona, *Managing Meetings* (Fontana, London, 1990).

Clemie, Susan and Nicholson, John, *The Good Interview Guide* (Rosters, London, 1990).

De Bono, Edward, *Mechanism of the Mind*, (Cape, London, 1969).

De Bono, Edward, *Six Thinking Hats* (Penguin, London, 1985).

Evans, Paul and Bartolomé, Fernando, *Must Success Cost so Much?* (Grant McIntyre, London, 1980).

Eysenck, Michael, *A Handbook of Cognitive Psychology* (Lawrence Erlbaum Associates, London 1984).

Handy, Charles, *Inside Organisations* (BBC Books, London, 1990).

Lock, Dennis and Farrow, Nigel, *The Gower Handbook of Management* (Guild Publishing, London, 1987).

Maddux, Robert, *Successful Negotiation* (Kogan Page, London, 1988).

Margerison, Charles and McCann, Dick, *Team Management* (Mercury Business Guides, London, 1990).

McKee, Victoria, *Working it Out* (Robson Books, London, 1991).

Mumford, Alan, *Developing Top Managers* (Gower, Hants, 1988).

Pascale, Richard, *Managing on the Edge* (Viking, London, 1990).

Pedler, Mike and Boydell, Tom, *Managing Yourself* (Fontana, London, 1990).

Peters, Thomas, *Thriving on Chaos* (Pan Books, London, 1988).

Woodcock, Mike, *Team Development Manual* (Gower, Hants, 1986).

Index

Solution to the Nine Dot Problem

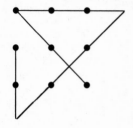